A HUNGER FOR HIGH COUNTRY

A Hunger for High Country

ONE WOMAN'S JOURNEY TO THE WILD
IN YELLOWSTONE COUNTRY

Susan Marsh

OREGON STATE UNIVERSITY PRESS • CORVALLIS

The paper in this book meets the guidelines for permanence and durability of the Committee on Production Guidelines for Book Longevity of the Council on Library Resources and the minimum requirements of the American National Standard for Permanence of Paper for Printed Library Materials Z39.48-1984.

Library of Congress Cataloging-in-Publication Data

Marsh, Susan (Susan L.)
A hunger for high country : one woman's journey to the wild in Yellowstone country / Susan Marsh.
pages cm
ISBN 978-0-87071-756-7 (pbk.) – ISBN 978-0-87071-757-4 (e-book)
1. Marsh, Susan (Susan L.) 2. Forest rangers–Wyoming–Biography.
3. Natural history–Wyoming. 4. Forest management–Wyoming.
5. United States. Forest Service. I. Title.
SD129.M234A3 2014
508.787092--dc23
[B]
2014023894

 First published in 2014 by Oregon State University Press
Printed in the United States of America

Oregon State University Press
121 The Valley Library
Corvallis OR 97331-4501
541-737-3166 • fax 541-737-3170
www.osupress.oregonstate.edu

I

ONE TASK WAS LEFT TO ME BEFORE LEAVING MONTANA, to bid farewell to Windy Pass. A gap along the crest of the Gallatin Range, surrounded by mountains and perfumed by wild phlox and lupine, it was among the places that offered refuge during the past six years, one that could be counted on to bring me clarity and solace. It was the place I needed now.

I climbed into the thinning air and the forest gave way to meadows and scattered clumps of whitebark pine. The air was crystalline that first week in July, too early in the season for the wildfires of 1988 to erase the view of mountains on all horizons. The kind of day that should have made my heart swell as I reached the crest of the Gallatin Range.

But the scenery only deepened my sorrow as I looked across Paradise Valley to the corona of summits of the northern Absarokas. Memories—of backpacking trips and day hikes and ski tours—lay heavy in my heart. I was moving away and I knew I would never climb those peaks again. I turned from the mountains to focus on immediate surroundings: the sweet floral scent that came in waves from the lupine; the native grasses, like horses' manes finely combed by a gentle wind. I dropped to my knees and forearms and pressed my forehead into the soft, forgiving earth, clutching tufts of alpine rush as if their wiry strength would hold me there. When I looked across the valley again the beauty was overwhelming, but something in me slammed shut like a metal door. After years of believing I had loved my job as well as that magnificent wild land, I saw the truth: I did not belong.

I meant to come to Windy Pass alone, but my final weeks in Montana were filled with packing boxes and attempting to sell the house that neither I nor my husband, Don, could bear to leave. As it happened, the local ranger district had arranged a tour of the Gallatin Crest Trail. My boss was not available that week, so Norm, the district's trail manager, called to ask if I wanted to join them. I understood the offer as a necessary gesture, acknowledgment that someone representing the supervisor's office should be included whenever the regional trail coordinator from Missoula was invited to the forest. The chain of command discouraged direct communication between a ranger district and the regional office staff, and with his phone call Norm revealed the breach of protocol that he was trying to repair. It was clear as well that he hoped I would say no.

"Sign me up," I said.

He paused. "Let me get back to you."

My phone rang a few minutes later.

"We have six people and six horses. Need one of them to pack the gear."

"I don't mind hiking."

Again the uncertain silence, during which I could have gracefully backed out.

"Okay then," Norm said. "We'll meet you at the trailhead at nine."

Not enough stock, no room in the district's vehicle. I knew the Windy Pass patrol cabin wouldn't accommodate all of us either, so I packed a tent.

It was close to ten by the time the six-pack pickup and horse trailer arrived, followed by Bobby Morton hauling his own horses. Wendell, the regional trails coordinator, strode toward me with a smile and an outstretched hand, while the others went to work sorting out saddles and bridles, brushing equine bellies and withers, and spraying insect repellent. Wendell and I moved upwind.

"So you're really leaving us," he said. He and I had talked often enough about the way things were at the forest.

"Not because I want to."

"Who's going to make sure the district doesn't piss away all this trail money they're shaking me down for?"

"I guess you'll have to do it."

He gave my shoulder a collegial squeeze and went to help pack gear. It was an excruciatingly slow process, and, assuming the horses would quickly catch up once the party got underway, I started for Windy Pass alone.

The trail began in the bright sunlight of a recent clearcut, where it was already close to eighty degrees. Welcome shade came at the edge of the cutover area, under lodgepole pines with thick, straight trunks and full crowns. An hour later I paused at an outcrop of volcanic breccia, its surface pocked with tiny holes where gas escaped from cooling lava. I looked down onto a patchwork of timber cuts and the narrow canyon of Portal Creek, tributary to the Gallatin River. The high peaks of the Madison Range soared above the Gallatin Canyon, their emerald wildflower parks at eye level from where I stood.

With no sign of the group behind me, I wandered slowly through the last of the lodgepole forest and into the open grassland below Windy Pass, dotted by clumps of fir and whitebark pine. When I reached the patrol cabin I left my daypack on the porch and continued on to the top. An acute ache grew in my throat as the sum of my situation that afternoon reflected the time I had spent in Montana: my separation from the group, the only one on foot, and—as usual—the only woman.

As a geology major barely out of my teens, I once looked around the classroom in math and physics courses to see few—if any—female faces. Instead of wondering why, I found some pleasure in the circumstance. I was a pioneer, smart enough to keep up with the boys in the so-called hard sciences. It had long been my ambition to keep up with the boys, from the time I was old enough to play with other kids unsupervised. Girls played inside with dolls, diminutive dress-up clothes and oversized high heels pilfered from their mothers' closets, or make-believe houses constructed from furniture and bed sheets. When television arrived in the late 1950s, both boys and girls settled onto living room floors to watch cartoons and B-movie Westerns. These activities bored me and I escaped to the neighborhood woods and fields. I loved to walk on the packed dirt paths, to climb high into the smooth-barked branches of Pacific madrone, to beachcomb aimlessly while my parents dug for clams.

For the most part, I played alone, unable to join the boys in their pick-up games of softball because I was a girl, unable to endure the company of girls if it meant being indoors on a sunny afternoon. I remember one small victory—shooting at a coffee can and (to my great surprise) actually knocking it over with the plastic bullet, when the boy who owned the toy gun couldn't hit it. A short-lived victory, as it turned out; after that, he wouldn't let me try again.

Later, I sought the friendship of boys, partly because they were funny and easy to be around, and partly because their sports had begun to mesh with mine. I was the only girl in my high school class who could keep up with them on skis, and the one whose counsel they sought when having girlfriend troubles. I reveled in being accepted as a friend since it was clear that I would never join the clique of popular girls. Nothing frightened me more than the prospect of dating, which was handy for someone who was never asked.

One day before the Senior Prom, the principal caught me hiding out in the art room during the pre-prom school assembly. When I told him I wasn't going to the prom and therefore preferred to miss the assembly, he stormed into the gym to berate the male segment of the student body. Reports from friends let me know that my name was used and for the rest of that week I slunk along the corridors for fear of some guy asking me out of pity.

I have often wondered about my fundamental affinity to the ways of males. I wore my hair long and even wore makeup for a time, and never wished that I had been born a boy. But I wanted to live like one, and be accepted as their equal.

By the time I entered graduate school I hardly noticed being the only woman in the room—it was something I took for granted. But in the Forest Service near the end of the 1980s, the lack of women among my colleagues angered me. Although I assured my non–Forest Service friends that the agency was becoming more progressive, it became increasingly clear that the opposite was true. I had witnessed a decade of backlash after court rulings required the Forest Service to hire more women. Some were treated with such resentment that they quickly found another path in life. For reasons I didn't fully understand at the time, I chose to stay.

While well aware of the challenges for professional women everywhere in the Forest Service, the clarity of the sky over Windy Pass that day shone new light on how I had contributed to my particular difficulties with a stubborn defiance and plain refusal to conform. My mind filtered out the good memories from nearly a decade with the agency and rendered a bitter cup of defeat. So what was I now preparing to do but leave a place I loved in order to take another job with the Forest Service, where I would always be a square peg? What made me believe things would be different in Wyoming?

I could not imagine a better way to spend my working life than as a steward of public land, contributing to the conservation of wild country held in trust for all. But the ingrained culture of a government bureaucracy sent my imagined vocation tumbling like a boulder down a talus field. I wanted to step into the lupine on the crest of the Gallatin Range and keep walking deeper into the backcountry, never to be seen again.

For natural resource majors in the 1970s, a reliable source of summer employment was the US government and its land management agencies. We surveyed for roads and cleared trails and cleaned campgrounds, spending our days outside in the beautiful wild places that attracted us to working for the Forest Service instead of wrangling burgers at a drive-in. Most of us had grown up hiking, skiing, riding, and backpacking, and physical outdoor work could not have been more natural. After the 1976 National Forest Management Act was signed into law, national forests were in need of planners to translate the high-minded legislation into science-based management on the ground. With my background in geology, landscape architecture, and environmental planning, this sounded like the job for me.

As a seasonal employee during the summers between my years of college, I had given no thought to gender politics or organizational hierarchy—as had been the case in high school, my male colleagues and I were classmates and equals, working together and having fun while we earned some tuition money. At the Fremont National Forest supervisor's office in Oregon, where I took my first permanent position, I found that gender mattered. Women filled lower-grade clerical and administrative positions; men were professionals and decision-makers. Having entered the Forest Service just before the door of opportunity slammed shut when President Reagan imposed a federal hiring freeze, I felt extremely lucky to have a job at all. I did my best to learn the unspoken rules of behavior as I navigated my lonely status as a professional woman: dismissed by male colleagues, resented by secretaries and clerks, condescended to by leadership. When the chance came to transfer to Montana after a couple of years in remote rural Oregon, it felt as though my dream position was being laid in front of me. I was headed to a university town in the Northern Rockies, employed as the forest's landscape architect. Montana had long glowed like a votive in my heart, from the time my parents and I visited cousins in Butte. At home, my parents were no longer happy with each other and seemed displeased with me. But the grin of pure pleasure on my father's face when a Bighole River trout took his lure set an indelible image in my mind. Montana was a benign and healing place, a place where I had family and to which I must belong. For the first time since

View north from Windy Pass, Gallatin Range, Montana.

I left my home of origin in the Pacific Northwest, there was no internal debate about the move.

When I arrived at the Forest Service office in Bozeman, I was warned of the preordained strikes against me: I was female, first of all. I had served as Federal Women's Program Manager while at the Fremont National Forest, which branded me a feminist. Second, I was a resource specialist, or *Ologist*, the category into which professionals other than engineers and foresters were lumped, hired to help implement pesky laws such as the National Environmental Policy Act, the Threatened and Endangered Species Act, and the National Forest Management Act. To these strikes I added a third, an ardent love of wild land and a tendency to share my perspective on how it should be treated, not always in the most delicate of terms.

I spent six years pushing back against an entrenched culture into which I did not fit, convinced that if the quality of my work was impeccable I could overcome the strikes against me. I refused to grasp the obvious, that individual excellence took a back seat to agency loyalty. Over the years I learned that acts of disloyalty included challenging unsupported assumptions made by the timber staff and having lunch in public with members of the environmental community—The Enemy. I lay amid the alpine rush and lupine at Windy Pass, fighting the flood of memories that clutched my throat and stung my eyes, relieved to have a few moments to gather myself before having to face the men.

Shouts and laughter alerted me to the group's arrival at the cabin below. I hurried down the trail to make myself useful.

But I felt no sense of usefulness as I approached the cabin, where the saddles were already stacked and blankets hung over corral rails, sleeping bags laid out on claimed cots, supper assembled and heating on the stove. I tried to join the rambling conversations but words didn't come and I hovered at the edges of the circle of men, where I was cheerfully ignored. The cord that tied me to that place had already been broken and I was looking through a thick pane of glass at a present moment that was already in my past.

The primary post-supper activity was trying to keep Bobby Morton's stallion from picking on the Forest Service geldings that shared the crowded corral. I couldn't be much help with that endeavor either, so I decided to wander back toward the divide in the lingering evening light.

Wendell had always treated me kindly and I considered him a friend. He gave me a quizzical look as I silently tied my boot laces.

"You doing all right?" he asked.

I wish I had taken him aside and let the stream of regrets flow onto his sympathetic shoulders. The events of the day had triggered a cascade of emotions, all of which had been my companions since childhood: shame, remorse, self-loathing. I was alone and unwanted, and would never fit in. But I couldn't speak and my eyes filled and I simply shook my head, thanked him for his concern, and walked away.

Madison River below Bear Trap Canyon, Montana.

2

THE WEEK BEFORE THANKSGIVING IN 1982, Don and I left our rented house in Lakeview, Oregon. Surrounding the northwestern corner of Yellowstone National Park lay the Gallatin National Forest, where I was expected to report to work the following Monday. We crossed Idaho's Snake River Plain as snow began to fall. Two anxious feline faces peered from the back window of my VW Rabbit, surrounded by house plants. Our Labrador retriever wagged his tail from the passenger seat of Don's VW bus. *Where are you taking us*, they all seemed to ask.

The snow increased as we drove eastward, and by the time we reached Idaho Falls tractor-trailers roared past through a foot of slush, engulfing us with their spatter and obliterating the roadway ahead. Wiper blades slashing, I used glimpses of their taillights to guide me. After we left the interstate the road began to climb and the gray of afternoon deepened. We stopped at the last service station in Island Park to buy chains for my car. The man advised us to take Raynolds Pass, a detour to the west, instead of going over the closer but more treacherous Targhee.

The mountains were socked in but I could feel their presence as we crossed the Continental Divide and dropped into Montana. The temperature dropped as well, and the pavement went from slush to black ice, with whiskers of snow swirling along the frozen surface like ribbons tied to a fan. My car shuddered under the force of shifting blasts of wind and the cats moaned in alarm. Beyond the fences that drifted in and out of view, knots of dark cattle stood with their tails to the storm. Vague shapes loomed and vanished and it was impossible to tell if they were farmhouses or mastodons. As the storm intensified even the roadside fences were absorbed, leaving a ghost of a landscape that was entirely imaginary. What I imagined was immense.

The road continued until I thought we would be blown forever across the high plains, ending up perhaps in Manitoba. How could a city of twenty thousand exist in the direction we were headed and, according to the map, be only thirty miles away? My thoughts skittered like brittle gusts of snow to news reports I had heard, of people stranded in their cars for days.

Past a battered, shot-up sign that announced the unseen town of McAllister the highway made a sudden right-hand turn and dropped into a narrow, twisting canyon. I slowed to a creep, grateful for the lack of traffic. Beside the road grew shrubby willows and tall reed grass. Lichen-splashed walls of dark bedrock rose from out of the willows and faded into the obscurity of the clouds. The rockscape was an abstract painting, a canvas of tortured, fissured stone ripped by deep cracks, its face a repeating pattern of blotches and pinpoints as the black and frost-green lichens merged with falling snow.

Without warning, the forbidding walls receded and the canyon released us. The quality of light, a perceptible brightening of the envelope of air as we emerged, spoke of a wider valley, the confluence of our little canyon with something major. The sign was plastered with snow and unreadable but I knew from looking at the road map that we were about to cross the Madison River. I had heard that name spoken in wistful and reverent tones by fly-fishermen from Washington to Utah. The legendary Madison, named by Lewis and Clark for Thomas Jefferson's Secretary of State who would later serve as the country's fourth president. Would James Madison be impressed or horrified by this namesake river whose black, choppy water now staggered drunkenly out of the mist? Whitecaps churned under the bridge, the water blown upstream by an Arctic wind. But on the banks of this unruly Madison in the middle of wild Montana, apparently oblivious to what we would later learn was a record-breaking storm, stood a half-dozen stoic forms, in a line along the riverbank like fence posts.

Fishermen.

I slowed to be sure of what I saw, a cluster of wool caps drawn down to meet the collars of heavy overcoats, long rods held at expectant angles, and a row of amiable faces. They shot me brief, not-to-worry nods that said there was nowhere these men would rather be. They let me know that I was now in remarkable country where I could expect to meet some remarkable people.

At that moment it occurred to me that I might be headed home. Since my teens I had longed for escape from the strip malls and airports and growing system of interstate freeways that were quickly obliterating any remnant undeveloped land in south King County, Washington. On weekends I found respite in the mountains an hour's drive from Seattle, where parts of the Cascade Range remained unspoiled. Like any other adolescent I did my time at the shopping malls, but even then their numbing sameness was evident and I yearned to break free. While others adopted mall strolling as a form of exercise, I hungered for wild places that offered renewal and discovery.

My adolescent dreams of future employment ran along the lines of becoming a lookout stationed in a lonely fire tower on a mountaintop. Having grown up with the lofty Olympic Range looming over Puget Sound and Mt. Rainier a stately presence on the opposite horizon, my thoughts turned naturally to the national parks. I had no concept of the differences among the various agencies that managed the state parks, national parks, and national forests where my family went camping. What mattered was the sharp, sweet tang of pines under a summer sun, the grin on my father's face when he had a fighting trout on the line, the tantalizing mystery of what lay beyond the next bend in the trail. Though we must have passed many signs that read *Snoqualmie National Forest*, the primary way of telling we were in a national forest was the lack of a grand entrance at which a ranger took our money and warned us not to feed the bears as he handed my dad a map. On excursions to the national forests, we left the highway and traveled along some nameless gravel road, sometimes climbing terrifying switchbacks, and suddenly we arrived—at the lake, the river, the campground. A beautiful, unexpected spot, apparently in the middle of nowhere. How did my father find it?

Among the books I spent hours with was Dad's copy of a thick guide published by the Washington Department of Natural Resources, describing every lake in the state that had been stocked with trout, complete with aerial photographs. The overhead views were of small, neat bodies of water shaped like pearls and teardrops, perched high above a great river valley among dark rocky peaks and snowfields. I wanted to visit all those wild lakes.

When I started to explore the backcountry on my own, I found it wasn't as wild as I had hoped. From lakeside campsites high in the Cascades the sunset views included a dun-brown pall of smog and a plain of distant twinkling lights. It included a spaghetti-bowl of logging roads that gouged the foothills and ended in square-mile blocks of clearcut forest. The wildlife I encountered consisted mostly of camp robbers and mule deer with a fondness for leftover instant pudding. At popular destinations like Mt. Rainier there were so many people and rules that no spontaneity was permitted, even in the backcountry. You had to reserve a designated campsite weeks in advance and plan your trip to be there on that day so you could pitch your tent among those of a dozen strangers. You had to register for a class and join the long line of guided parties to climb The Mountain. If you were young and unaccompanied by parents, the rangers eyed you with suspicion and reminded you that loitering was not allowed. The Freedom of the Hills read the enchanting subtitle of the first mountaineering book I bought. Freedom—where was it?

Don and I found a house to rent among the hayfields at the edge of Bozeman, a half-hour walk from the Federal Building and my office at the Gallatin National Forest headquarters. At the end of November it was dark when I left for work, and by the time the sun rose I was sitting at my desk. I had spent my first week on the job organizing a corner cubicle between disbelieving glances out the window. From the expanse of glass beyond my drafting table stood the Bridger Mountains, a rugged spine of limestone and snow-flocked forest that rose from the outskirts of town and humped its way northward to spill into foothills at the edge of a nearly uninhabited prairie. Being able to look out my window and see this kind of view reinforced the notion that I had found my dream. I was amazed at my good fortune, even as I sorted through the broken chairs and equipment with vital pieces missing, the detritus left after my predecessor retired and his office was plundered for anything of value.

Joe Gutkowski still lived in Bozeman, and I met him soon after I arrived.

"It's about time somebody showed up," he said. "I was afraid they weren't going to fill the job at all."

"How could a forest like this get by without a landscape architect?"

"It's been close to a year since I retired." His black eyes snapped. "Took the bastards twenty years to get rid of me. But the second I was eligible, I was out of there."

My boss later confirmed that Joe had retired soon after his fifty-fifth birthday, following a career of smoke-jumping, forestry, and landscape architecture. A career spent in the woods, at what must have been exciting, high-risk jobs—my wildest imaginings did not include jumping out of airplanes into forest fires. But at fifty-five, strong and vigorous as most twenty-year-olds, Joe couldn't wait to leave his job. He punctuated his words with laughter and arm waving as he briefed me on some of the reasons why.

"One thing you have to know is that this forest is run by foresters and engineers. The last thing they care about is scenery. Everybody's got some hare-brained idea for how to improve the forest—this road, that timber sale, and pretty soon they've got it carved up and looking like hell and running all the elk out of the country." He shot me a devilish grin. "I fought them every inch of the way."

We exchanged phone numbers. I thought the conversation was winding down, but Joe was just getting started. He regaled me with stories of arguments that ended in fistfights and examples of how he had taken matters into his own hands when district rangers failed to do the right thing. He cut illegal fences that barred access to creeks and burned illegal cabins deep in the backcountry.

"Two of the district rangers put me on notice that I wasn't allowed on their turf without permission!" He seemed delighted, as if this was a mark of honor. "Naturally, I was there the next day."

By the time Joe and I parted I was more than skeptical of some of his stories. How could he get away with all that fence-cutting and cabin-burning without being fired?

"People didn't always agree with Joe," a timber staffer told me later. "But he cared intensely for the forest, and people respected him for that. He meant what he said."

Like Joe, I meant what I said, and I could not imagine how being honest might bring trouble, assuming I did not resort to fistfights. I resolved to keep my mouth shut and my ears open, good advice for any new kid on the block. I had already gotten a hint of what lay ahead when I was introduced to my colleagues in the supervisor's office. The forest hydrologist, a quiet man whose diction was polite and vaguely British-sounding, had caught wind of the fact that during my tenure as Federal Women's Program Manager in Oregon I had assisted employees in filing civil rights complaints. Before I could say hello he asked if I was a bra-burner. Decades later, I am still too flabbergasted to think of a snappy comeback—perhaps I could have told him that I hadn't owned (or needed) a brassiere since I threw out my training bra at fifteen. But he had delivered important information, not only about the status of women at the time but the power of the rumor mill. My application for this job had been thoroughly discussed, and conclusions about me had been reached, weeks before I set foot in Montana. Why did this surprise me?

My next task caused some apprehension after the conversation with Joe. I made introductory calls to the ranger districts, five geographic subdivisions of a two-million-acre national forest that included terrain from the windswept northern plains to the highest mountains in Montana. When might I arrange to see the district and meet the staff, I asked, and did they have any projects for which they needed consultation before the snow got too deep?

"We're already using snow machines down here," the voice in West Yellowstone said. "Bring your lunch and we'll spend a day riding the trails."

I penciled the date on my calendar and looked forward to my first ride on a snowmobile, then I dialed the district office in Gardiner. How about tomorrow, the ranger said.

After scraping frost from the windshield I drove the eighty miles to Gardiner, site of the historic Roosevelt Arch at Yellowstone's north gate. On that first drive through Paradise Valley, where the Yellowstone River ran north from Gardiner between rows of bare cottonwoods, I saw within the space of ten minutes a pair of bald eagles perched on a cottonwood snag, a herd of elk crossing the highway, mule deer browsing among the junipers on a mountain spur, pronghorns working their delicate paths through a stand of sagebrush, a cow moose in a willow flat, and a band of bighorn sheep standing on a limestone cliff. I swelled with the anticipation of adventure: those mountain ranges flanking the valley and striking the sky with their spires were part of the Gallatin National Forest—my new workplace.

By the time I reached Gardiner I had nearly forgotten this was a work trip; I was being paid to sightsee. Soon afterward I would learn that most of the wildlife I spotted on the far side of the Yellowstone River found their winter ranges on a private ranch, the new headquarters of a California religious cult. The center of controversy for the next decade, the Church Universal and Triumphant had purchased from billionaire Malcolm Forbes a splendid cattle ranch sandwiched between the river and Yellowstone National Park. Joe had filled me in on the national forest's negotiations with The Nature Conservancy as the federal government had attempted to purchase the ranch for a wildlife haven. The plan fell through at the last

Old growth Ponderosa pine, Fremont National Forest, Oregon.

moment, in part because the government could not offer as much money as the church could. On receiving news of the ranch's sale, the forest's lands manager in Bozeman had laid his head on his desk and cried.

At the Gardiner Ranger District I was greeted by a woman with graying blond hair, a tanned face full of wrinkles, and dark, friendly eyes. She led me down a hallway to a collection of map tubes and mismatched file cabinets where half a dozen employees gathered at a folding conference table over day-old doughnuts. Veiled eyes assessed me from under cowboy hats as I stood there in my Birkenstocks. The district ranger was a tall, florid-faced man with sun creases at the corners of his eyes. He had the long arms and large hands of a farmer. When I held my hand out, he declined to shake it.

"Hi," he said without a trace of warmth in his voice.

He must have been one of the rangers who had banished Joe. His sharp blue eyes challenged me and I took a long deep breath and held it, along with my practiced smile.

"Where you off of?" someone asked. Forest Service parlance for *Which forest did you come from?*

"The Fremont."

Blank looks and vague nods.

"Region Six—Oregon," I said, glad that at least I'd understood the question. I had worked *on* the Fremont National Forest; now I was *off* it. Unlike employees of the National Park Service who were stationed *in* national parks, US Forest Service employees worked *on* forests. This habit of speech still sounded odd to my ear, and a bit alarming when I first heard it applied to someone who was away from the office for a fire-fighting assignment. Blandly the secretary said, "He's on fire."

The district wildlife biologist had heard of the Fremont.

"I remember that place," he said. "Isn't there a district at Bly?"

At last, a conversation starter, a point in common with one of my new colleagues. I waited for him to ask if I knew so-and-so.

"Bly, Oregon," he said as he reached for a stale doughnut. "If the world needed an enema, that's where it would go."

In spite of my initial trepidation, I knew that I would love Montana. My office window framed snow-clad peaks and buckskin colored foothills in the low November light. The country that was now my place of work included famed trout streams whose names alone were enough to set my former college professors into a swoon, the highest peak in the state at nearly thirteen thousand feet, and endless hiking and cross-country skiing out the back door. Ross, my supervisor, who covered both recreation and public affairs for the forest, was a kind-hearted forester of the old school, which expected hard work and dedication and getting out into the field where hands and jeans had a chance to get dirty. He had grown up in upstate New York and had worked for the Forest Service since graduating from Paul Smith's College decades before. But the Forest Service was changing and the new ways left him flabbergasted. Instead of scribbling a memo on a legal pad and handing it to a clerk-typist he was expected to type it himself, on a computer. Instead of getting his jeans dirty in the field (the field being Forest Service lingo for the forest itself, though the Gallatin had few actual fields within its borders) Ross was increasingly stuck behind a desk. It was clear that he had more to do than one person could handle, and spent his days embroiled in public controversies: timber sales in grizzly bear habitat, a massive high-end ski resort proposal (also in grizzly bear country), and controversy surrounding the forest plan.

Ross delegated to me aspects of the recreation program that he didn't have time for. These included backcountry and wilderness, which he said needed some attention. I took on these unexpected duties with delight.

3

IF A PASSION FOR FOREST RESOURCES EXISTED at the supervisor's office it was kept well hidden. The life drained from people's faces as they entered the Federal Building and stood waiting at the elevator. Some days it felt as though robots walked the hallways, eyes glued to whatever stack of paper they carried as they passed, as if it held urgent and important information. It must have been the building, I concluded, with its sterile walls and polished vinyl floors, long fluorescent lights and windows that didn't open.

The supervisor's office in Oregon was unassuming by comparison. Most people wore jeans or their field uniforms, and some sat at their desks in hardhats and overalls. The building stood on the edge of town, with the national forest directly behind it. The Ologists—all of them men, representing scenery, watershed, wildlife, range, and soils—sat together in one corner of the office they called the bull pen, and spent a good measure of their office time counting down the days before goose season. The silviculturist jogged during lunch breaks and came back to the office in his shorts. He was a proud member of the NURDs—North Umpqua Road Dashers—a group of Forest Service colleagues who met for races and fun runs on weekends. He was as likely to laugh at himself as everyone else in the office, and he even laughed while arguing over a timber sale with one of the Ologists before asking him to join him for a beer after work. The 4:31 Club met daily at the OK Corral (good sandwiches) or the Round Up (dusty two-headed calf in the window, bring your own glass if you want a clean one).

In Montana, a sense of distrust permeated the office. While jeans were still the norm among the Gallatin National Forest staff, they were clean and sometimes even pressed. Cowboy boots were polished and lacked manure under the heel. The office was perched on the third floor of the tallest building in Bozeman, with only a distant view of the forest.

Left: the author at her desk in the supervisor's office, Bozeman, Montana, 1985.
Right: Joe Gutkowski, retired Gallatin National Forest landscape architect.

I soon learned that it was more than the setting that contributed to the office atmosphere. Whispered warnings came from colleagues, usually after I had offered my unsolicited opinion. Watch your back, be careful what you say, look out for so-and-so. The doors of staff officers were often closed and arguments bordering on shouting matches could be heard from within. Newbies like me were a threat, the public was a threat, and no one had better question a pronouncement from top management.

I asked Joe how district rangers got away with telling him he needed their permission before he set foot on "their" district.

"Most of the time they were blowing smoke," he said with a laugh. "They know they can't keep me off public land. Their problem with me was I caught them being sloppy. One let a cattle rancher build a road into an area that's been proposed for wilderness. No analysis, no public involvement, just get on the bulldozer and go do it. I went up there to have a look and found the road was right in the creek. I was hopping mad and blew the whistle on him."

Joe laughed louder. "He must have got chewed out because right after that he called to tell me to stay the hell off his district."

I had not been given the same edict—yet—but I could see it coming. A few days earlier I had had a disturbing encounter. I was writing scenic protection standards for the forest plan, the guiding document that would govern forest management for the next twenty years. As part of my task I visited each of the five districts so the rangers and their staff could offer assistance in mapping what we called visual quality objectives. VQOs ranged from Preservation, under which no landscape-altering activity could be done (and applied only to designated wilderness), to Maximum Modification. The VQO assigned to each parcel of national forest directed the degree to which the landscape could be altered by road-building, timbering, or any other ground-disturbing project. I already knew from past experience that rangers in particular resented such restrictions. Under pressure from above to meet timber targets, they wanted to "keep their options open"—a phrase that had become a mantra.

This desire for flexibility resulted in part from the changes washing over the agency at the time. Demands on the Forest Service to provide more of everything—timber products, wildlife habitat, trails and campgrounds, and wilderness areas—coincided with increasing budget constraints. Environmental laws passed during the seventies were only now being implemented with final regulations, all of which were written by USDA staff, interpreted by legal experts in the Forest Service's Washington office, reviewed by the public and committees of scientists, rewritten, and finally sent down to the forests as reams of *Thou Shalts*.

When I arrived at the district whose ranger would not shake my hand, there was no staff assembled in the conference room. I started to explain what I'd been doing with the other districts as I unrolled a table-sized map.

"Doing this your way isn't going to give me enough flexibility," he said.

"It's not *my* way," I said. "It's national policy."

He waved me off. "I'll map the VQOs for this district myself. As far as I'm concerned, you can go home."

I could think of no response but to leave the map lying on his desk and do exactly as he directed.

The society of a national forest is a caste system. The top tier consists of the forest supervisor and district rangers—the "line officers" in Forest Service parlance, who make the decisions and sign their names to those decisions. The primary staff officers give specialized advice to the supervisor. A rung below the staff and rangers are the hopeful, earnest rangers-in-waiting, who live to earn favor with the higher-ups and spend most of their time at training or making presentations at forest leadership meetings, gaining "visibility." The rest are worker bees, divided into professional, administrative, technical, clerical, and wage-grade classes. For communication and direction a militaristic chain of command prevails in which the worker bee and forest supervisor exchange information through several ladder rungs, often with the message diluted or omitted.

Beneath the recognized castes lay informal subclasses of employees: the harmless and widely tolerated drone class, men near retirement who sat at their desks cracking jokes and talking about elk hunting. The idealistic but disenfranchised group of professionals who occupied positions thrust upon an unwilling agency by the need to comply with environmental laws. Wildlife biologists, soil scientists, landscape architects, and archeologists, we were the troublemakers who questioned every given pearl of wisdom and challenged every proposal. It was our job to do so, but that didn't win us favor among the foresters who were used to running the show without having to explain themselves. A favorite editorial cartoon of the time went up on several office doors, featuring a man in an agency uniform, bound and gagged, with the caption, "The latest endangered species—the big-mouthed biologist."

"Keep in mind the way you're treated is not your fault," the Federal Women's Program Manager told me over coffee. "This forest has a totally hostile work environment, especially for women."

"How's that possible?" I asked. "Look at this place . . ." I swept my arms toward the window that framed the majestic Bridger Range, as if doing so said it all. What I meant was that such a magnificent place could only attract the best. And the workplace didn't seem all that hostile to me, though after encounters with rangers who wouldn't shake my hand and planners without a sense of humor, perhaps my standards were too low.

In reply Candace cited her own situation. She was a cartographic technician but her job was quickly changing with the advent of computer-based geographic information systems and the level of specialized knowledge they required. "I have a degree in geography and have been trying to get out of the tech series for two years. I get nothing but brick walls, no help, no explanation, while some of the guys are getting promoted. I have to conclude that management simply doesn't want any more professional women here."

Sara, a wildlife biologist, had been sitting quietly and chuckling at my incredulity. A professional with a PhD and many years of experience, Sara had applied for a downgrade from her previous position because she wanted to relocate from southeastern Idaho to Bozeman.

"I didn't even make the cert," she said with a bitter laugh.

How a grade-11 employee with a doctorate and years of experience as one forest's lead biologist failed to make the list of eligibles for a grade-9

Sara Johnson at Windy Pass, Gallatin Crest Trail, 1986.

position at a ranger district was among the questions Sara asked when she filed a formal civil rights complaint. While her complaint was being processed the job she had applied for was filled by a nice guy from Alaska who had no idea what he was stepping into. After Sara prevailed in her complaint the forest had to invent a new position and offer it to her.

"They've hated me ever since," she said.

The plain truth of it was that Sara had been blackballed. She'd been too successful at her previous forest, doing her job as an advocate for wildlife. She was a woman, of course—she had that strike against her, especially in the eyes of the previous forest supervisor whose religion dictated that women work at home. Sara was smart and highly educated and scared the socks off of many of the men who had risen to leadership positions with bachelor's degrees. And she wasn't afraid to take them on.

Candace and Sara were by no means the only ones who felt wronged by the Forest Service culture. It was not always about gender. Over the years I've known more men than women who left the agency in a state of bitter discouragement, and some of my new officemates were to be among them. Six people occupied what was once the supervisor's office conference room, now with a placard reading *Recreation* above the door. For lack of space elsewhere, Sara and her boss, the forest biologist, shared one corner of the room. Trying to survive until he was old enough to retire in a couple of years, Jerry, the biologist, stuttered and stooped as if perpetually expecting a whipping. The lead fisheries biologist (also known as the fish head) was a jovial team player—no timber sale was too close to the creek, even if it was in the creek—and so he got along, at least on the surface. But getting along and getting by seemed to be the most he hoped to accomplish. Across a burlap-covered divider from the fish head sat a wizened and angry range conservationist who chain-smoked at his desk, forced to take a downgrade by some bygone reorganization. Also sharing the office space was a young part-time archeologist who reported to me, prehistoric sites being a subset of recreation according to the Forest Service. Ann held a master's degree in anthropology and a black belt in Aikido. Our eclectic group was compatible enough, and we gave each other glances of sympathy as the lack of privacy allowed us to follow the fish head's divorce, the range con's slow asphyxiation, and lectures delivered to the biologist by the forest supervisor.

Most of those monologues addressed the biological opinions to be written regarding the effects of proposed roads and timber sales on grizzly bear habitat. The forest supervisor would end the conversation the same way each time: "We need a no-effect call on this one, Jerry." He turned on his heel and left the room as Jerry lowered his eyes and stared at the top of his desk.

My heart went out to Jerry and his sense of defeat, but it was hard to blame Supervisor Drake for the situation. Like the rangers, the forest supervisor had a target to meet, and meeting targets was goal number one. Each fiscal year when the funds were doled out to the forests, a list of expected outputs went along with them. Some were considered "hard targets"—the millions of board-feet of timber to be offered for sale being primary among them. The target was taken seriously and the only acceptable excuse for not meeting it was a catastrophic wildfire that required everyone to drop their regular work and help. So-called soft targets included measures such as the number of campgrounds managed to standard, the number of archeological sites inventoried, and miles of trails maintained. No supervisor would miss the chance at a promotion for failing to meet his trail target. The timber target was another animal altogether. Western states' congressmen, acting on behalf of the timber industry that helped put them in office, routinely pressured the Forest Service to increase timber harvest levels.

Forest resource specialists were expected to help meet the timber target even if the evidence suggested that a proposed sale and road construction would harm wildlife, scenery, water quality, or soil. Those who went along and caused no trouble were tolerated; the others were not. Beyond the standard expectation that the Ologists sprinkle holy water on timber sales, it was likewise understood that you were either "one of us" or "one of them." The categories of "them" were numerous and ever-shifting so it was hard to know how to avoid being cast into the wrong group. One thing that was sure to place you in the *them* column was being a wiseass. Young college grads who found entrenched protocols ridiculous, clerks who bristled when treated like servants, and the occasional Ologist whose spouse made a living that could support them both if necessary made up the majority of this group. The wiseasses questioned authority, sneered at the jargon-laden press releases issued by the public affairs department, and delighted in pointing out inconsistencies between what was said and what was done. Naturally, these were the people who drew me.

Read any history of the Forest Service and you can't avoid the references made by old timers to the Forest Service family. People would take you in when you were stranded in a strange town, and greeted you like an old friend at a regional meeting. Where spouses and children lived together at remote work stations, the Forest Service was literally an extended family, with wives taking care of matters at the compound while the men spent their days afield.

The same histories will tell you about the way the family atmosphere began to dissipate with the push to recruit resource specialists and "diverse" employees. Diversity was defined in terms of ethnicity, not attitude. Newcomers were expected to embrace Forest Service mores of thought and behavior, for the downside of the esprit de corps within the agency was a slavish allegiance to conformity. Those who had grown up in the family understood the way things worked, often at a level so intuitive they couldn't explain what made working for the Forest Service different from simply having a job. With a crop of new hires brought in by environmental legislation, consent decree, and national civil rights initiatives, resentment was inevitable. As one of my colleagues grumbled after a contentious meeting, "It's hard to be a team player when you're not wanted on the team."

The so-called diversity employees rode the roughest trail, for they were often quite alone with no support system. Diversity sounded great from the distance of Washington. DC, but in the Rocky Mountain West the reality was harsh. It meant being the first woman ranger in a town full of cowboy hats, the only African-American within a hundred miles. These employees worked long, hard hours to prove themselves in the face of severe loneliness and constant reminders of their difference. Well-meaning locals asked where they were from, the implication being *Not from here, certainly*.

Most newly hired Ologists were ignorant of the agency's chain of command organization and the trade-union basis of traditional positions. The early Forest Service was heavy on technical jobs that did not require a formal education. Drunks were pulled off bar stools and handed a shovel when men were needed to fight fire. Leadership positions from district rangers to the chief of the Forest Service were filled by men who worked as technicians for years, graduated forestry school, and began at grade-5 in the general series (GS) employment structure of the Office of Personnel Management. They learned their trade as GS-5 junior foresters and were promoted when eligible to what were called "journeyman" positions at the GS-9 and 11 levels, a process that could take years. Many friends of mine retired at the GS-11 level and were glad to have achieved that rank.

Enter the Ologists with graduate degrees, hired as GS-9s and 11s due to their advanced education. We lacked understanding of Forest Service culture and soon learned that our education was of little help in the on-the-job training for The Way Things Are Done. It was easy to see how a GS-7 forester who had been hoping for a promotion might resent us.

"You have nothing to worry about, you're respected here," Ross told me. I wanted to believe him. But that morning Sara had angrily reported that the deputy forest supervisor, at a meeting of the forest's rangers and top staff, had referred to the three of us—Sara, Ann and I—as "Ross's crack crew."

I thought the Gallatin deserved to be the jewel of the national forest system, but budgets didn't keep up with need and I was often incensed at how the district rangers chose to spend what scant recreation and wilderness funds came their way. One hired a wilderness ranger who spent the summer staining bunkhouses and had been in the wilderness twice; another used its entire trail budget to fund the summer fleet—vehicles used by campground hosts and timber marking crews. It became my crusade to right these wrongs, and Ross used to joke about how I hammered away at the rangers until they did what I asked. I might have been naïve but I knew this: the last thing a district ranger wants is some busybody in the SO telling him how to spend his money.

4

ONE MORNING TOWARD THE END OF WINTER I asked Ross what he knew about the Bear Trap. I had heard the name in conversation and it had taken me a little while to realize it was something other than a tavern with a historic-sounding name.

Ross looked up with the smile of someone who had just gotten good news about an old friend. "I float that section all the time. You need to go."

He unfolded a forest map and his finger traced the lower Madison River.

"I remember that place," I said. "When I was coming from Oregon there was a blizzard blowing sideways across the road and it was just about dark. I saw people out there *fishing*."

He laughed. "That was probably me."

"So, what about this trap?" I envisioned a box canyon with a headwall that couldn't be climbed, even by an agile black bear.

Only the name of a tributary creek, it turned out. Local geographic features in that part of Montana had long been given names of enigmatic origin. You knew there was an intriguing story but no one remembered what.

Ross knew one story about the Bear Trap: he told me to look for the ruins of a cabin on a mining claim three miles upstream from the highway. "Old guy used to live alone up there. He was cleaning his gun and accidently shot himself in the leg."

I gave him a look that said no one cleans a loaded gun.

"I know," Ross said. "Anyway, he could see he was about to bleed to death so he lit a signal fire and it got a little out of hand. He ended up burning the place down."

The old man was rescued, as it happened, but without the need to give him access to his cabin, the Bureau of Land Management closed the road and now it was a popular trail.

"Improved the hell out of the fishing when they closed that road," Ross said. "If you go past the first couple of miles, you have the river to yourself."

On a clear March morning Don and I drove along the winding strip of asphalt, past a monochromatic landscape of bare tilled fields and straw-brown pastures. Farmhouses with brushy shelter belts appeared in each draw and pale Charolais cattle basked in the early sun, their faces tilted to the east like rows of sunflowers. The same cows, I guessed, that I had seen with their hindquarters to the wind the day the storm blew us into Montana.

No trace of the November blizzard remained; after two weeks of subzero cold around Thanksgiving, the winter had turned mild and dry. January had given us days above freezing and clear nights well above zero. No snow had fallen on the valley floor for weeks.

Beyond the dairy farms and undulating prairie the road curved sharply to the south at a spot known to the Montana Department of Fish, Wildlife and Parks, which maintained a wayside there, as Crapper Corner. There, the Madison River unfurled from its canyon. Dark blue and choppy with wind, it rattled over black boulders. A bridge came into view ahead and a wooden BLM sign read *Bear Trap Canyon Recreation Area*. We turned onto the narrow dirt road and followed the river upstream. Above the banks lined with tall reed grass the dry, open slopes rose to the canyon's edge in a mosaic of grass, brush, and scree. Aspens crowded the hollows where a thin crust of snow curled away from the late winter sun, its surface gray with dust. Mahogany, juniper, and limber pine dotted ribs of bedrock between the draws. Boulders blocked the road beyond a patch of grass and cobble where a single car was parked. We pulled in beside it. The map posted on a signboard showed a trail all the way to the Ennis Dam powerhouse, about eight miles upstream, a considerable day hike leading deep into forested backcountry.

We started up the trail, not sure we wanted to see the burnt cabin. After hearing its story, I felt I was entering a haunted place, even if the old man had survived. The haunted feeling came partly from the dark water, the shadowed canyon walls, the black timber climbing toward the mountains. Though the air was mild, the dark metamorphic boulders we passed were cold. We pushed through curtains of bare willow stems, noting the stalks of poison ivy along the trail.

A fisherman stood beside the river just beyond the willows.

With friend Karen, at the confluence of Bear Trap Creek and the Madison River, 1986.

"Any luck?" Don called.

"Kinda slow."

I knew from years of greeting fishermen that "kind of slow" meant he hadn't had a strike all day. "Not too bad" meant that everyone in the party had caught a limit.

An hour's walk from the trailhead, Bear Trap Creek tumbled down the eastern flank of the canyon. Tall cottonwoods marked the confluence where we found the cabin site, now a heap of charred timbers, rusted nails, bedsprings, and broken glass. People had camped in the cottonwoods nearby, using the remains of the cabin for benches.

Beyond the ruin the trail disappeared into a thicket of willow. We found a tiny patch of sand beside the river to have lunch and I bent to dip my fingers into the ice-cold water of Bear Trap Creek. When I reached into the Madison River with my other hand it felt strangely mild. The geysers of Yellowstone, fifty miles upstream, warmed the river even here. We ate our sandwiches to the music of blended waters. The mild air held tiny midges and a promise of spring. Already the aspen catkins had started to bulge with silvery white heads, and the buds of mock orange and chokecherry looked ready to burst, with green showing between their brown bud scales like the hems of petticoats. As if feeling the season, Bear Trap

Bear Trap Canyon of the Madison River, 1983.

Creek splashed over a tangle of shifting boulders with the high-pitched chatter of an excited child.

Just over a mile from Bear Trap Creek the trail left BLM land and entered the Gallatin National Forest. Immediately a sense of responsibility sharpened my step and I paid more attention to the condition of the trail, noted any small campsites we passed, and scanned the forest floor for litter. This "busman's holiday" condition was common to many Forest Service employees, especially seasonal backcountry rangers and those responsible for keeping campgrounds clean. You enjoyed your hike on a day off, but you didn't ignore what needed to be taken care of.

After we crossed into the national forest, the cliffs of dark gneiss soared higher above the river and the canyon walls rose so high they left only a sliver of blue overhead. Fallen rocks began to clutter the Madison River's flow, and we could hear rapids upstream. The sound drew us into an open forest of old-growth Douglas fir. We heard a canyon wren singing from across the river and caught a glimpse of a small flock of migrating mountain bluebirds darting in front of the black bedrock faces like confetti that fell from the sky.

We hiked as far as the canyon's largest rapid, the Kitchen Sink (named for the one item not thrown at a boatman by the Madison River), before the day's light began to fade. I stood before the whitewater roar as it clattered off the canyon walls and planned future trips into side canyons, down the river, and up mountains on the far side of the river. The Bear Trap was a snow-free refuge from Montana's months of winter, a place one could walk on dry ground any month of the year.

For the rest of the winter the weather remained dry and mild, and Don and I spent nearly every weekend exploring both sides of Bear Trap Canyon, bunchgrass slopes and plateaus above the river, and downstream until we ran out of public land and the bright-orange paint on fence posts warned us away from private ranches. On fifty-degree days when the wind was calm we paddled sections of the river, amazed to be using the canoe in March. I never lost the sense of foreboding that accompanied my first entrance into the canyon, but the Bear Trap also seemed welcoming, a new extension of a widening home.

The view from Crapper Corner was dominated by Red Mountain—a hill, really—1,300 vertical feet above the valley floor. It stood on the west side of the Madison, its shape reminiscent of an armchair upholstered in the plush pastel of short bunchgrass stubble. We found a place to park at its base and hopped an unmarked barbed-wire fence to begin the climb in a narrow boulder-choked gully. A warm wind stirred from the southwest, sending mare's tail clouds pinwheeling across the sky and combing the river's surface into whitecaps. Prickly pear cactus and soapweed yucca grew with Indian rice grass, evidence of the area's aridity. The outcrops of ancient metamorphic rocks held specimens I had seen only in college laboratory collections: a pegmatite of clear quartz and rose-pink feldspar, some of it broken to reveal an on-end view of interlocking crystals known as graphic granite. I traced the *M*s and *L*s and *S*s in wonder. Perfect "books" of twinned biotite clusters opened from dark schist, each page easily loosened with a fingernail. Red garnets the size of fingernails studded a bed of sand-colored granulite. Everywhere the rocks told of a long and complex past in the language of foliation, lineation, partial melting and crystal zoning, intrusive dikes and secondary pegmatite veins. I later learned that these were among the oldest rocks in the region, at 2.8 billion years.

The junipers looked as old as the rocks, some of them two feet thick at the base. The diversity of leafy flowering plants, though still in winter's dormancy, would surely call us back in a few weeks' time. Mountain and curl-leaf mahogany, mock orange, wild rose, serviceberry, and chokecherry packed their stems into deep fissures in the bedrock, seeking hidden nutrients and moisture.

We followed a spur ridge out of the gully and surprised a pair of coyotes on their morning patrol. Rocks clattered above and we looked up to catch a half-dozen mule deer deserting their roosts in the mountain mahogany. Tracks and droppings wove a lacework under the mahogany and junipers; the deer had spent the winter in this draw and had slowly begun moving up the mountain with advancing spring. Their trails passed under a cliff holding a red-tailed hawk's nest, where a lost arrow joined the interwoven branches.

Above the outcrops at its base, Red Mountain opened to the sky. The bunchgrass that had looked like sheared velvet from the road turned out to be widely spaced on a slope covered in shattered rock. I glanced across the barren face of the mountain and spotted a patch of intense magenta-pink, looking as if a surveyor had spray-painted a rock. As I approached I saw it was a wildflower and all at once I saw them everywhere, bowls of silver-green leaves holding flowers packed so closely each resembled a chalice full of wine. I got down on all fours to fill my view with the season's

Boundary sign for the newly designated Lee Metcalf Wilderness, 1984.

first wildflowers, in bloom before the vernal equinox, not an inch above the surface of the ground from which they summoned tiny flies. *Douglasia montana* graced the slope in ever-greater profusion as we wandered from plant to plant in a state of wonder and enchantment.

The slope gentled near the top and we left behind the *Douglasia* to walk upright along the summit ridge. A rock cairn as tall as I was marked the apex and as we approached a Bald Eagle took wing from behind it. We dropped our day packs and sat against the sunny side of the cairn, facing the Spanish Peaks. The Madison River was an ink-blue ribbon emerging from the cleft of Bear Trap Canyon. To the north lay miles of gently tilting prairie. In the hazy blue distance we could make out the headwaters of the Missouri River, the place where Lewis and Clark first laid eyes on the ring of mountain ranges surrounding us. The rising Missouri still looked about the same as it must have to the Corps of Discovery. The Spanish Breaks, the rumpled hills between the high mountains and the broad plains of the Madison and Gallatin Rivers, were marked only with a few widely spaced cattle ranches and we could not see Interstate 90 or the defunct smokestack at the Trident cement plant near the town of Three Forks. The Trident plant had been closed for years and the railroad along the Jefferson River had been converted into an equestrian trail. Fishermen used it to hike into spring creeks where fat brown trout lurked. Horsemen rode from Lewis and Clark Caverns into downtown Three Forks, where the bars still had hitch rails beside the parking lots.

How different this landscape—high, arid, with plants and animals I had never seen—was from the Pacific Northwest forests I had loved as a child—yet, the Bear Trap became a refuge in much the same way, a place I got to know by heart during hikes on and off the trail, where I imagined secret places that only Don and I knew. The Bear Trap was one of many little-known pockets of wild country that I adopted as my own, all of them wonderful and unique. Yet I understood that they stood in for the five-acre patch of second-growth forest where I played as a solitary child.

Not long after I became acquainted with Bear Trap Canyon, Congress acted on a long-standing wilderness proposal and the canyon was included in the Lee Metcalf Wilderness, named for the late Montana senator who championed preservation of wild lands in the state. Since most of the 5,000-acre Bear Trap Canyon unit of the four-part wilderness was administered by the BLM, five square miles of the area within the national forest were transferred to that agency. It was the BLM's first (and, thirty years later, only) wilderness in Montana, and for that I felt glad, while wistful that I could no longer consider the canyon part of my workplace.

I once heard a story that the Honorable Mr. Metcalf, having consumed a little whiskey, punched out one of my least-favorite politicians in an elevator. I was never able to verify the legend, but after hearing it, I thought I would have liked Lee.

5

MY FIRST FEW MONTHS IN MONTANA were those of slumber for hibernating bears, a time when backcountry travelers could ski or snowshoe in a state of relaxation rather than one of hyper-vigilance. I remained vigilant, having never lived in a place where an encounter with a grizzly bear was more than a half-imagined possibility. I could not bring myself to admit it, but I was nervous around—that is, afraid of—bears.

When summer burst through spring's weeks of fog and snow squalls I began to explore the national forest in earnest. I would hike alone for many miles as long as I was north of a line that glowed bright in my imagination: occupied grizzly bear habitat. When I ventured over the line toward Yellowstone National Park, it was always in the company of others and preferably on horseback. Camping meant hours of wakefulness in the tent and startling at every snap of a twig. I didn't know enough about bears, other than their status as the subject of controversy, so I sought the company of those who did.

On a mild Saturday near the end of June, seven people gathered at a trailhead in the East Pioneer Mountains for a weekend excursion sponsored by the Montana Wilderness Association. New to the area, and interested in what this conservation organization was all about, I talked Don into something we rarely did—hiking with a group of strangers. A couple from Butte was already there when we drove in and we shyly introduced ourselves. Their golden retriever wagged his tail and sniffed our legs. Bruce, a professional wildlife photographer from Kalispell, joined us soon after, and soon the trip's leader, a burly blond man who called himself Wag, skidded his old Dodge pickup into the gravel. One beefy hand grasped the steering wheel and in the other he held a bottle of Henry Weinhard's. An illegible tattoo smudged the skin over his bicep. He looked more like an aging Hell's Angel than a Forest Service landscape architect. But he was my counterpart, the forest landscape architect for the Beaverhead National Forest, and one of the first people I met in Montana. He had urged me to join him for this weekend trip to the Pioneers so he could show me some real wilderness.

A Subaru with Bozeman plates was the last vehicle to arrive. The woman at the wheel peered at Wag from behind her dark mane of hair as she cautiously approached. She rolled her window down an inch and looked around the wide spot in the road that served as a parking area. Ours were the only vehicles there.

"Is this the Wilderness Walk?"

All of us were thinking, *What else would it be*, but we politely nodded. I couldn't tell if her weak smile signaled relief or disappointment. She parked and introduced herself as Ruth, and immediately began questioning Wag.

"There aren't any bears around here, are there?"

Wag smirked and drained his beer.

Ruth pushed on. "I know it's silly, but I am scared to death of them."

"There's bears. Probably won't see one here, though. Not a grizzly, anyhow."

"I hope you're right."

Grizzly bear patrolling a willow bottom.

Wag reached into the bed of his truck and pulled out another Henry's. "Don't worry about bears," he said. "There's about two hundred left in the whole state."

Ruth and I exchanged glances, hoping for reassurance in each other's eyes. Newcomers from opposite coasts, we had signed up for this backpacking trip to meet people, see new country, and pitch our tents where a bear was unlikely to wander through. None of the maps I had seen of occupied grizzly bear range included this part of the Beaverhead National Forest.

"Last October was the last time we got a report of a grizzly around here," Wag said. "We'd be lucky to see one."

Bruce brightly put in that he'd be thrilled to see one. A veteran of photographic expeditions deep in Glacier National Park, he was accustomed to seeing bears, and perhaps they were used to seeing him.

We hefted our packs and headed north along a gentle trail to the Twin Lakes Basin. The crest of the East Pioneer Mountains lay ahead, visible where the trail crossed wet meadows and disappeared. We looked for blazes across the meadows and usually found one, and I was glad for a trip leader who knew his way around this barely trailed country.

The larger and deeper of the Twin Lakes lay no more than three miles from the trailhead, and we had our camp set up by lunchtime. The couple from Butte threw a stick into the lake for their dog to chase. Ruth was content to sit in camp and read, and since she was afraid of bears, Wag offered to stay with her. With most of a June afternoon ahead of us, Don and Bruce and I decided to climb to the crest of the range, directly above the lake, and hike to Highboy Mountain.

I had seen the Pioneers from Interstate 15, and while they looked intriguing from that distance, they struck me as a minor range compared to the hundred-mile-long chain of the Absarokas and other mountains closer to Yellowstone. The hike from Twin Lakes showed me my ignorance. The crest, at well over ten thousand feet, was gentle and grassy on its west slope, while on the east, the bedrock faces, carved by glaciers, plunged steeply into talus slopes, moraines, and basins filled with snow. Lakes dotted the break in slope where the rugged mountains met the forest. In June, snow still hung among the crags, and blocks of ice floated in the lakes. We hiked a mile and a half to the top of Highboy, from which the view of the other high peaks of the East Pioneers was magnificent. Sawtooth Mountain stood directly north, pale folds of unraveling rock on its west slope, snowclad cliffs on the east. The conical summits of Mounts Tweedy and Torrey, the highest in the range, stood across a wide basin from Sawtooth. Lakes in various stages of thaw glittered in high sunlight. Below Highboy's cliffy east side, a wide rock glacier had pushed Chan Lake into a skinny comma of deep blue water ringed by snow. Wag had said the grizzly bears had been seen in these mountains, and they were known as one of the last redoubts for wolverines in this part of Montana. In spite of logging roads and impoundments for irrigation water, these mountains remained wild.

Bruce stood on the top of Highboy with a tripod and camera until cumulus from a building thunderstorm darkened the sky. We had no rain that afternoon, but the clouds lent the dark rock of the mountains a somber aspect as we retreated down the ridgeline to Twin Lakes.

Hours later, awake in my tent as the full moon shone through the fly, I imagined a bear behind every tree.

The few wild bears I had encountered usually sprinted away before I realized what I had seen. Only once, in Wyoming, had a bear failed to bolt. Don, his sister Harriet, and I nearly ran into it on a trail in the northern Wind River Range. It followed as we retreated to a talus slope and scrambled onto the largest boulder. The bear circled, closing in until it was only thirty feet away. It stood on hind legs for a better look, raised its nose in our direction, and ambled a few steps closer. Its face was broad and concave, characteristic of a grizzly. We clapped our hands and hollered. Don blasted a dog-training whistle, making the bear wince and flatten its ears. Finally, it lumbered down the trail—in the direction we planned to go.

We quickly changed our plans. We marched back up the Palmer Canyon trail, across a high plateau, and back to the headwaters of the Green River. At dusk we arrived in the grove of spruce where we had camped two nights before. Yeah, I told myself—no unreasonable fear of bears here. In the Pioneers I was determined to prove myself braver than Ruth, who had recently arrived in Montana from New York City.

I did not realize I had slept until I sat up, suddenly awake. Something felt wrong. I listened for noises but nothing stirred. I stuck my head out of the tent's zippered door to check on the food bag, hung high between two lodgepole pines. The meadow, the draw where the creek ran, and the talus slopes lay in their proper places. But the moonlight drained them of familiarity and benevolence, rendering ghostly images in black and silver. Under my straining eyes, shapes at the far edge of the meadow appeared to jerk and twitch, as if an animal moved among the willows. The moon's position above the western skyline told me it was long into the night.

Bear claw marks on an aspen.

Through the treetops the Big Dipper teetered on its handle. Ursa Major—the Great Bear. I hoped the only bear I saw that night was the one that hung above me in the sky.

I closed the tent flap and slid back into my bag, filled with a vague sense of dread. Don's watch, dangling from a mesh pocket in the side of the tent, read 3:00. Too early to get up, I pressed my back against my husband's warmth and catnapped until the light that hit the tent fly came from the rising sun.

On Monday morning I arrived at my office in Bozeman. A note lay on my desk, penciled in Ross's hasty scrawl. "Gone to West—bear incident." I ran downstairs for a newspaper.

The headline leapt at me. *Bear Kills, Eats Camper.* At Rainbow Point, a popular campground on the outskirts of the town of West Yellowstone.

Mid-afternoon when Ross returned to the office, I stood at his office door. His body sagged, his face was drained. He slumped heavily into his chair and sighed.

"You don't have to talk about it," I said.

He handed me a stack of photographs. A ripped tent. Pine saplings smeared with blood. Ross sighed again and seemed to be fighting stomach sickness. With his eyes fixed on a point across the room, he stared past the half-eaten chocolate doughnut that had lain on his desk since early morning. I looked at a few more of the pictures. Dizzy and nauseated myself, I handed them back.

"The guy was doing everything right," Ross said. "No food in the tent, even his toothbrush was stashed away. The campground was full of people."

"Did they find the bear?"

"Not yet. But we've got all the campgrounds emptied and closed. Every motel room in West Yellowstone is booked."

"When did it happen?"

"Saturday night. Around three in the morning."

I whistled softly. The same hour I sat up in my tent in the Pioneers, not many miles away.

Biologists found the bear sleeping off its meal in the cool mud of a willow bottom near the Madison River. It was killed and brought to Bozeman for examination. What had prompted an apparently healthy grizzly bear to enter a crowded campground and pull a man out of his tent as if selecting a sandwich from a vending machine? The biologists had no answers for the newspapers.

"We couldn't find anything wrong with the bear," one researcher said. "But this is very unusual behavior. Bears will avoid people unless cornered or injured."

While the biologists scratched their heads, the Forest Service armchair experts offered theories. Most agreed that Yellowstone grizzlies had become aggressive because they were not hunted.

"We need a season on these bears so they'll remember to be afraid of people," one of my colleagues growled. "I never go out without my rifle. It's too bad they didn't clean out the bears a hundred years ago."

Joe was angry over the bear's death. "This was their home first. With the roads and campgrounds and open dumpsters all over town, it's a wonder there are any bears left around West Yellowstone. We ought to stay out and leave them alone. Without the grizzly bear, there is no wilderness."

For what was left of June, the vague apprehension I had felt in grizzly country bloomed into rampant paranoia that nearly kept me out of the mountains. I stayed far north of Yellowstone, peering into the forest as I walked and listening with every step. I crept, rather than hiked, the strong opinions of friends and coworkers playing over in my mind. Many people expressed great passion for bears, and a fierce desire to protect a creature that could kill and eat them. Others, just as passionate, would prefer to be rid of them.

The bear looming in my mind, fed on legends and lies, was surely larger and more fearsome than the Yellowstone grizzly. But even in Montana, where people claimed to know better, bear lore consisted of tall tales. No one ever came home from an encounter saying, "I saw a grizzly bear today," as if it were a bluebird. There was always a narrow escape, a harrowing scramble up a tree. Hearing these stories made me consider any bear a threat. Now one bear had confirmed my deepest fear. For days after, the light-headed nausea that swept over me when I flipped through Ross's blood-smeared photographs still clung like cobwebs in a darkened closet. I might be eaten.

Before Don and I moved to Montana, a friend gave us a book, *The Grizzly Bear*, written in 1909 by William Wright. One evening after the attack at Rainbow Point, I took the book to the backyard hammock and read until twilight.

During his twenty-five years in the company of wild bears, Mr. Wright evolved from trophy hunter to naturalist. He wrote, "I studied the grizzly in order to hunt him. I came to hunt him in order to study him. I laid aside my rifle."

Wright began his career by hunting what he saw as a ferocious predator, the bear of the imagination. After years of observation, he discovered a largely vegetarian creature, smart and resourceful and worthy of respect. He ended his book with the conclusion that grizzly bears were defensive, not aggressive. They did not go looking for trouble, but avoided it if they could. The same thing the biologists were telling us now. But Wright's grizzlies lived in the Selkirk Range of northern Idaho, an entirely different ecosystem that bred apparently gentle bears. What would Mr. Wright have made of the bear at Rainbow Point?

In 1983 grizzly bears in the northern Rockies seemed intent on proving experts wrong. The summer had scarcely begun, and already they had mauled hikers in Glacier National Park and raided dumpsters in Cooke City. They were killing domestic sheep by the dozens in the Absaroka Range. And now one had pulled a tourist from Wisconsin out of his sleeping bag for a meal. If these bears weren't looking for trouble, what were they up to?

Like people, bears were unpredictable. I couldn't tell the shy ones from the killers, so my reaction was to assume the worst about them all.

Two-year-old grizzly cubs eating biscuitroot.

Yet they fascinated me as rare emblems of the wild. Wherever I found signs of bears, I knew the land was big enough, wild enough, to sustain the rest of the wildlife that belonged there. Yet I still held the unconscious assumption that I stood at the top of the food chain, able to walk down a trail without fearing for my life. The grizzly bear made me consider what I was really asking for, when I asked for wilderness. The only parts of Montana without grizzlies were those from which they had been eliminated. My preference for hiking in those bear-free zones made me wonder—did I agree more with my coworkers who thought all grizzlies should be shot than I did with my conservationist friends? Did I want a forest cleansed of dangerous predators, made safe and sanitized? I didn't think so; I liked seeing old claw marks on the trees and piles of scat full of berries. But I wanted to keep my distance. I hoped the bears would keep theirs too.

In my hammock, and at the Montana State University library, I kept reading about bears. The grizzly resisted my attempts to comprehend it. It retained its mystery even to the experts, despite the radio collars and maps of its migrations around the Yellowstone region. The grizzly was a singular, different sort of creature, ready to disprove whatever we concluded about it. Still people sought human-like, or at least understandable, behavior in the bear. What we hoped to find was kinship. I recalled from photographs that a bear, when skinned, looked especially human, curled like a sleeping child. It looked too much like us not to share some of our traits.

Grizzlies once seemed like big friendly dogs, begging doughnuts from tourists and sidling up to the garbage-dump "lunch counters" in Yellowstone. In those days, people knew the bears as simple creatures looking for a free meal. With the dumps long closed, the bears were wild again, and once again ineffable. The one I had encountered in the Wind River Range of Wyoming stared with tawny, inscrutable eyes. In them I tried to read familiar urges and emotions. When the bear turned around at last to leave us, its gait suggested nothing so much as boredom. But my attempts to read its gestures did not alter the reality of the bear, a bear beyond my knowing. For many moments I stared down the trail to where it vanished, before I slid off the boulder and marched the other way.

I began to read beyond biology, searching for the bear of myth and literature. I found that the grizzly bear had starred in stories as ancient as humanity. Surprisingly, the storied bear was often depicted as a transformative healer, the giver of life. The bear, in its hibernation, brought forth new life each spring, a creature of beginnings and rebeginnings. A creature signifying not death but resurrection.

Perhaps the bear offered a model for profound change. Who, after all, did not feel changed after a close encounter with a wild grizzly bear? The one that had me scrambling up a boulder in the Winds remained vivid in my mind for years. A creature that could brand its image upon me asked a question—what part of myself was I seeking to avoid? What inner transformation did I fear?

By encountering bears in the forest, in the newspapers, or in the ancient myths I was transformed from a blithe recreational hiker to wary potential prey. Because of the bear I began to see the forest with new eyes, eyes that had reason to stay alert. I came to notice the snap of a twig, a dark shape in the shadows, and understand what these might imply. Though the experience was not pleasant, it brought me closer to being part of the wild.

After the hike with Wag in the Pioneers, I joined the Montana Wilderness Association, and as a membership gift I received a belt buckle. I opened the box to find a bronze grizzly bear looking back at me. Around the bear's face curved the words, "Montana Wilderness." As Joe had said: the bear, the wilderness—one and the same. Included in the box was an invitation to a potluck for new members in Bozeman.

When I arrived, Ruth waved from across the room. I found a plate and helped myself to elk stew and a brown, savory biscuit. As I sighed with pleasure at the first warm bite, a bearded man with sandy gray hair grinned.

"Like those?" he asked.

"They're wonderful. Did you make them?"

"My specialty. Grizzly biscuits."

I pondered this for a moment. "Why do you call them that?"

"Secret ingredient. Grizzly bear fat."

I smiled. Surely he was kidding.

"Dan guides for an outfitter in the Yukon," my hostess whispered. "They hunt grizzlies. He brings back enough lard for a year's worth of potluck biscuits."

I began to eat the biscuit more slowly, though not with any less pleasure, trying to discern the taste of grizzly bear in the rich, sweet flakes. Eating of the bear, like some forbidden fruit, inspired both thrill and unease. Did eating of the bear lend me any of its spirit? I did not feel braver or stronger after one biscuit, so I reached for another. Somewhere in my body there were cells absorbing bear grease, molecules of grizzly becoming part of my own mantle of fat. Would the next bear I encountered in the forest sense that I had eaten grizzly biscuits? Would it be angry, or afraid?

I worried that eating of the bear might make me its enemy. Television nature programs from my childhood, with their footage of lions running down gazelles, had instilled in me the idea that predators were always the enemy of prey. Remorse began to intrude on my enjoyment of the biscuit. I did not want to be the enemy of grizzly bears. I wished the hunter in Canada had missed his shot, and that this bear remained a bulky shadow in the forest.

A few weeks later I was in the field with the district timber staff and biologist, looking at a proposed timber sale in a stand of lodgepole pine a few miles west of Rainbow Point. I started into the dense forest of lodgepole pine while they stood at the truck perusing a map. Knowing I was trespassing in bear country, I practiced an absurd combination of stealthy walking and loud singing. Many of the pines around me wore long vertical gouges left by claws. I wore my bronze belt buckle like an amulet, as if this display of solidarity with the bear might offer some protection.

Though I would have felt more comfortable among trees with fewer claw marks, I walked for reconciliation. This was the bears' home before it was mine. This was wilderness, complete with its predators. Under the canopy of pines roamed lynx and fishers, wolverines and grizzly bears. Wolf tracks had been seen on the plateau above. Somehow, we had to hold this complete, priceless wilderness together. How could a timber sale help? Once again I found myself in the position of defending the wild in my heart while my job demanded that I participate in designing the timber sale so that it would not mar the landscape. The district wildlife biologist had already blessed the project, since more sunlight on the forest floor would encourage huckleberries. I hoped he was right.

Like the wilderness, the bear survived because enough people held wildness in their hearts. Though we feared the grizzly when it came too close, we feared more our power to extinguish such a creature. Wag had said that by the early 1980s only two hundred grizzly bears remained in Montana. Every year there were more people. Though part of me feared them, I knew the bears had more to fear from us. Through inattention or willful destruction, we had already extinguished too many other creatures, too many other wildernesses. In the region surrounding Yellowstone, people's voices gathered: *Don't let it happen here.*

Living in bear country tapped a tattoo into my brain: even at the outskirts of Bozeman I kept our garbage can in a shed and glanced toward the apple trees and garden whenever I walked outside at night. I paid attention as I walked in the forest, knowing that I trespassed, knowing that the landlord might be observing my progress. Like a lodgepole pine with deep parallel grooves running down its trunk, my life was marked by the presence of bears.

From myths and science, knowledge and experience, a new picture of the grizzly bear emerged in my mind. Each image was a thin vellum overlay, a translucent sheet through which I could see the others. When I peeled back the vision of a brute on hind legs swinging its head menacingly, I found a gentle bear sitting on its haunches eating berries. They were the same bear: threatening and benign, feared and revered. The Yellowstone grizzly minded its business, resisting the human intrusions at its door.

In 1909 William Wright lamented, "When my grandfather was born, the grizzly had never been heard of. If my grandson ever sees one it will likely be in the bear pit of a zoological garden."

Nearly a century later, Wright's grandson could still see a wild grizzly bear in Yellowstone. The old man would be pleased to know this, I thought. As I continued through the forest, I paused at each claw-marked tree, fingering the pitchy scars. Like beacons they announced, more powerfully than the bright blue marking paint a pre-sale forester had overlain upon them, *Here wild bears still thrive, to dig roots and catch spawning trout, to mate and den and bring new cubs into the world. To feed our imagination and dreams.*

The sharp crack of a twig jerked me alert. I froze in place and strained to hear, boring into the shadows with owlish eyes. From an alder-choked gully came the snap of branches breaking. My pulse pounded in my throat and I glanced around at the trees in case I needed to climb one. What if I had chanced upon a cub, whose mother was nearby? How stupid of me to be walking in this place, out of earshot from the others, beyond anyone who might come to my rescue. The thrashing in the alders continued, but I could not catch a glimpse of a moving branch or the blur of a running animal. Probably just an elk, I said aloud, while images of half-eaten bodies and saplings slick with blood flooded my head.

I stood still as a doe until the sound vanished into the forest. I never saw the bear.

6

ON A HOT JULY MORNING I skimmed along the Buffalo Horn trail on a borrowed horse to a lake perched a few hundred feet below the crest of the Gallatin Range. Trash patrol was my purpose. Ramshorn Lake was situated in a sort of no-man's land, within a Forest Service wilderness study area but also part of a state-owned section and not specifically the Forest Service's responsibility. Once, that had not mattered: some forest ranger thought an outhouse was needed and installed it; others had cleared the trail. But the state of Montana was an absentee landlord and Forest Service patrols had lapsed. Campers were not cleaning up after themselves.

The director of the student outdoor program at Montana State University had been the latest person to complain, and he wasn't concerned about whose land it was. "Somebody needs to get up there and take care of it," he said. I promised that I would.

I rode with Nancy, the Bozeman District's recreation manager. Sal, my Palomino mare, tailed the rump of Nancy's white Appaloosa, the four of us on a girl's trip. I wanted to pinch myself awake: I was riding into a wilderness lake on a smart, fast-stepping horse with tall wildflowers dusting their pollen on my jeans and mountain ranges unfolding before me. The seven-mile climb, farther but more gradual than the trail to Windy Pass, seemed effortless. Perhaps Sal saw it differently, although her smooth, eager step suggested she enjoyed it too.

Before I got my first glimpse of Ramshorn Lake, we found the campers' communal dump at the base of a mammoth spruce tree: a mountain of crushed tobacco tins, empty gallon cans of Coleman fuel, and vegetable cans with peas on labels faded to an unappetizing pale blue—as if even the label had gone to mold. We dismounted and surveyed the heap. Far too much for the two of us to haul out, but we could at least gather it into trash bags for a pack string to pick up later. We tied our horses and donned work gloves.

The dump's discarded artifacts revealed a stratigraphy of time. Fresh steel flashed from the top of the heap and grew muted with rust and spruce needle duff as we worked our way through it. The bottom of the pile held items that looked vaguely familiar but were no longer seen on grocery store shelves. I recognized the faded corner of a red-and-white plaid label from a brand of strawberry jam my mother used to buy. Before I took a bite of my peanut-butter sandwich I would give the Wonder Bread a gentle squeeze and lick off the bright, sticky jam that oozed out.

I found the rusted shell of a small, square can with a tiny spout, the kind that might have held a half-pint of maple syrup. I turned it upside down and peered inside, as if to coax the last dribble. It was packed with cobwebs, dirt, and twigs. Peeling the fragile skin away, I held a sort of fossil, the perfect rectangular cast of a syrup can, rendered in forest debris.

We stuffed trash into black garbage bags until we filled a half-dozen, then we stacked them like leaf bags under the spruce and tied a note on each: "The dump is closed. Please pack out your trash. Thank you, USFS."

By the time we finished it was early afternoon and time for lunch at Ramshorn Lake. We found the perfect sitting log, facing a bay of shallow water that lapped over amber-colored sand. The horses, relieved of their bridle bits, crunched at the lakeshore sedges, oblivious of the view. Across the lake, where tall spruces leaned over the water, the water deepened to emerald, then sapphire, and a trace of pollen swirled across its surface in curlicues of pale yellow, an ever-changing design formed by the shifting breeze. The forest that grew here had little to do with the forest that once was. We could see its remnants in the rhyolite cliffs above. Petrified logs and tangled roots of magnolia and gingko glinted from the dull gray cliff face below the crest of the Gallatin Range.

"What a gorgeous spot," I said, unnecessarily. And added, thinking of the trash we had recently packed up, "Too bad people don't appreciate it."

Nancy asked what I meant.

"All that crap."

She thought for a minute. "At least it was all in one pile."

She had a point, I supposed. In the few weeks since snow released its grip on the backcountry I had gotten to a few other popular backcountry lakes like Ramshorn. No mounds of discarded tin cans such as the one we had found here, but plenty of litter and fire rings stuffed with melted glass and blackened steel cans. I had become so obsessed with cleaning up that I sometimes forgot to stop and look at the view at all. It seemed an occupational hazard to acquire an eye only for trash. More than once I had bent into the shadows, about to pluck a delicate wild rose blossom, mistaking it for a wad of Kleenex. Inch-wide facets of silver mica had stopped me on the trail until I saw they were not gum wrappers. At meetings in the regional office in Missoula I had met employees from adjacent national forests who proudly told me about their successful efforts to keep trails cleared and campsites free of trash, with the support of their supervisors and the help of a sensitive and compliant public. From what I had seen so far in the local area, "my" forest was far behind.

My zeal for trash-collecting extended to the front country as well. One day while at a campground with the Bozeman district ranger, I found a neatly tied trash bag that had been left near the vault toilet. Aluminum cans clinked softly within as I swung it into the back of the pickup. On the way down the Gallatin Canyon we started smelling something, not quite like old road kill, but every bit as foul.

"It seems to be following us," John said.

I checked the soles of my boots. Cracking the windows didn't help, but on the long drive back to Bozeman it began to dawn on me that the source of the stink was the trash bag.

"You know," John said. "That biffy just got pumped. When people throw trash into the vault the pump can't remove it."

The pumping contractor must have left that bag for later retrieval. On the outskirts of town we found a dumpster and the ambience in the pickup's cab improved remarkably.

At Ramshorn Lake Nancy and I sat quietly, she apparently content in the silence and me bursting with questions.

"What kind of education program do you have?" I asked.

She took a while to answer, as if wondering if I was inquiring about the school district. "Sometimes teachers ask us to give a presentation. Mostly it's about fire prevention."

"Any backcountry patrols?"

"Not really."

She paused as if about to continue, but then fell silent. I rushed in to fill the quiet behind her words, suddenly hungry for conversation. I babbled for a while about the great wild country and how I liked living in Bozeman, but the anger I could not hide crept through—didn't it make her mad to see a beautiful backcountry lake like Ramshorn treated like a garbage dump? Not only did I fail to imagine tossing my trash into the trees after camping, I couldn't consider it acceptable in my job as a forest manager.

"Anyway—don't mean to rant," I said, catching myself too late. "I'm glad to have someone as supportive as Ross for a supervisor."

She made a noncommittal sound deep in her throat when I mentioned Ross and I glanced at her with a question in my eye.

"He didn't support me for this job," she said.

"Why not?"

"I don't ski."

In Ross's world an effective recreation manager on a ranger district that included Bridger Bowl and Big Sky resorts needed to ski. It was part of the job, just as it was part of the job to pack a horse and back a trailer.

"I'm signed up for ski school this winter," Nancy said. "Not that I really want to go."

"I'd be glad to cover the inspections for you," I offered.

She didn't take my offer as seriously as I'd given it. Though the prospect of alpine skiing didn't thrill her, she would have to learn. It was expected.

I told her about a conversation I had had with a group of Forest Service people after a recent meeting, when we gathered at a West Yellowstone eatery over beers.

"What was the worst job you ever had?" somebody asked.

No one hesitated. "Swamping pig stalls." "K.P. during basic training." "Scrubbing pots in a basement kitchen in Aspen." Around the table, many forms of drudgery were reported.

I had been a bean-and-blueberry picker at fifteen (saving money, as I recall, for a new pair of skis), and followed that with a succession of grunt jobs: kitchen help at a retirement home, fountain waitress, hotel maid.

Nancy gazed across the still lake. "I've liked all my jobs," she said.

I found her comment hard to read. Was she telling me my conversation bored her? Had I asked a question that struck her as too personal? I had known people who never had a bad word for anything or anyone, which seemed admirable at first but grew to grate on my nerves. It was as if they had no opinions at all. But I liked her, and wanted to get to know her. The safest topic seemed to be the work at hand. I stood.

"When do you think we can get this out of here?" I asked, referring to the trash bags.

She said she wasn't sure.

"Any chance of getting the trail crew? I can help too."

"Maybe, but they work for Norm."

Norm was in charge of roads and trails for the district, the one who had hoped so fervently that I would turn down the offer to ride to Windy Pass. His shoestring trail crew, a man and a woman, were enthusiastic lovers of the backcountry.

"But Norm works for you, right?" I asked.

She shook her head and in her lack of further comment I read that not only did he report to someone else, he probably didn't often ask her about what she wanted done in the trails department. Finally she said, "It's pretty much a guy's district."

"We'll figure something out," I said, and let it go at that. I found her manner impenetrable, for unlike Ann and Candace and Sara, she seemed to hold no personal passion or point of view. Even her laugh was muted. She accepted without question the gender inequality within the forest and the degraded condition of the lakeshore we visited. I felt a personal, if not professional, responsibility to the condition of the lake, but in Nancy's presence, I began to question my motives. I was an advocate for wild country, and believed my passion was helpful in the business of conserving public land. If guided only by emotions, one could step beyond the limits of professionalism.

It wasn't until much later that I understood that my discomfort around Nancy went far deeper than our surface differences. She reminded me of someone, and eventually I realized it was the wife of one of my professors in graduate school, a small and quiet woman in her forties. Her husband, a fierce ex-Marine, dominated conversation in their home. She was smart—an intellectual, in fact—but her manner was one of a repressed woman, cowed into submission. I liked my professor for his strong opinions and offbeat sense of humor, and I wanted to like her just as much, but she gave me no material to work with. Like Nancy, her way of getting along exacted too high a price—the stifling of one's soul.

I did not get along well as a child. I wanted to play outside, and found that in order to do so I would have to play alone most of the time. The kids in my immediate neighborhood were a year or two older or younger than me, an enormous difference at that age. As we entered our teens, their interests changed, while I was still climbing trees. I abandoned Campfire Girls when the group stopped going hiking and camping. Outdoor activities were replaced by monthly meetings in someone's living room, receiving instruction on how proper young ladies should behave. I learned how to remove the white gloves I would never wear again, gently working loose one finger at a time. I learned how to make a casserole of green beans, sliced hot dogs, and crumbled potato chips. The message was clear: the time in my life for playing in the woods had passed.

I chafed against the expectations of my culture, yet I saw the need to get along if I wanted to be accepted. Caught between two disparate parts of myself, I left my adolescence primed for a Forest Service job. The back yard woodlot where I had spent my childhood as a tomboy had been cut down for a subdivision and I never stopped grieving for it. The growing distance between my parents sent me toward other adults, early mentors who took their kids skiing and backpacking.

MEN WANTED read a 1905 recruitment poster for forest rangers. "A ranger must be able to take care of himself and his horses under very trying conditions; build trails and cabins; ride all day and all night; pack, shoot, and fight fire without losing his head. . . . It is not a job for those seeking health of light outdoor work . . . Invalids need not apply." This was the Forest Service of the olden days, the one Ross could relate to. I admired it too, and found nothing discriminatory about it, given the era.

In the more recent time of Equal Opportunity Employment, the Americans with Disabilities Act, and mandatory civil rights/diversity training for every USDA employee, the verbiage of the century-old poster now brought a snicker or a sigh. The Forest Service had been slow to grow out of its rugged-male roots. In 1905, it was assumed that only men were capable of laborious outdoor work, though by 1913 things had already begun to change. That summer, Hallie Daggett was hired as a lookout on Klamath Peak in California. Her colleagues bet she wouldn't last the season, but she remained for fourteen years.

As time passed, more women were employed to cover clerical tasks when the paperwork got deeper than a ranger could handle on his own, and by World War II women served in many capacities, including field-oriented jobs. The ranger's wife had a special role as an unpaid administrative assistant and social coordinator for the isolated compounds where Forest Service families found themselves living in close quarters. But to be the ranger herself, and by the 1980s a few women were, that was a horse of an entirely different color. The agency had trouble adjusting to women in leadership positions, especially when some of them were not particularly suited to the job. Any woman appointed to a professional or managerial position was said to have gotten there simply because of her gender. It was said about both Nancy and me when we took up our new roles for the Gallatin National Forest. In spite of the circumstances, the fact remained that we were employed as resource professionals, my task to revive a moribund backcountry program and Nancy on her way to becoming a district ranger and probably forest supervisor. This was progress, wasn't it?

After lunch we inspected the ring of campsites that circled the near shore of the lake like a mud necklace. Trees had been reduced to hacked-off stumps, each one perched on a pedestal of exposed roots with the soil around it eroded into the lake. The remains of the lakeside forest weathered from the earth like the petrified root balls jutting from the cliffs above. Heaps of scorched cans and melted beer bottles lay in the campfire rings. The shredded remains of a blue tarp festooned a juniper. We each took another garbage bag and started back to work.

Ramshorn Lake, despite its distance from the trailhead, looked like the ultimate party spot, and the Forest Service's standard plea to "leave no trace" had made little impression here. Regardless of that, I picked each scrap of foil out of the fire rings, believing that if the area was cleaned and cared for, the next people to come would treat it better. If neglect fostered more of the same, the opposite must also be true. Perhaps, if I did my job well enough, I could fuel someone's fantasy that he or she was the first person to behold this mountain lake. I imagined the family that would come, perhaps with a child of nine or ten, that age when everything in the world still seemed magical. She might remember the excursion as the time they discovered ginkgo trees made of agate, weathering out of the cliffs, an azure lake that shone like a jewel. Even the fossil syrup can, which I had left sitting upright on a log, would be part of a child's imagined history. To a ten-year-old, something so old might as well have belonged to Lewis and Clark.

Clink. Another half-melted Miller bottle settled into my trash bag.

"It's three o'clock," Nancy said. "We'd better be going."

We slouched in our saddles on the way down the trail, listening to the rattle and clank of bottles in two of the smaller garbage bags we were able to tie onto our saddles. I sang all the songs I knew that included the name Sal, tossing my voice between the horse's ears. They flicked backward whenever the mare heard her name. As we descended the slope of the Gallatin Range a storm built over the Spanish Peaks. A steely wind sliced the sun's warm breath and the aspens began to murmur about anticipated rain. Distant thunder boomed and the wind picked up, blowing dust into our faces as we reached the trailhead.

"How can I help?" I asked, as Nancy expertly trailered and grained the mares.

She didn't suggest a useful role for me so I stood aside and watched the storm and wondered what she thought of me. Confident and quiet, at home with the stock and willing to strap on unfamiliar skis, accepting whatever was required, Nancy had what it took to be a successful woman in the Forest Service. Wisdom lay in keeping one's head down, or in Ross's words, "lying low in the brush."

I wasn't one to lie low in the brush, and I longed to make a difference. The week before, I had reviewed a proposed timber sale high in the northern Gallatin Range. Walking through a stand of grouse whortleberry and whitebark pine, I asked the forester, "This can't be commercial timber."

He looked puzzled. "We think it should sell."

I didn't have an answer. My question was less about the likelihood of someone bidding on the timber than the loss of backcountry in a pocket of forest so high it was close to timberline. Growing only above eight thousand feet, whitebark pine was an emblem of high country. The stand where we walked reminded me of places I had backpacked.

"How do you know it will grow back?" I asked.

"It's a productive site. We can make it look all right, if that's the concern."

He was sincere, and interested in reassuring me that there would be no repeat of the square cable units in Bozeman Creek that were visible from town. When snow lay on the ground the evenly spaced clearcuts looked, in the words of the forest timber staff, like diapers on a clothesline.

I should have offered this forester my own reassurances that I could help design the cut units to blend with natural openings, for my only task in regard to that timber sale was to help retain the scenery. But I brooded over it, feeling more like an accomplice to an execution than a manager of the forest, betraying the wild country that had meant so much to me. I'd known too many patches of doomed forest, starting with the one I'd played in as a child. Each one stood in for all the threatened remnants of the wild continent that I had been unable to save. I gave a few suggestions about "visuals" and said nothing more about my unease. A newcomer to the Forest Service, I sought the balance point between speaking my mind and retaining enough credibility to be heard.

Gallatin River from the lower Porcupine Creek Trail, 1985.

Gallatin River Canyon, 1985.

Nancy had come to terms with the political realities of the job. For her, acquiescence was a small price to pay for working in such country as was ours, for getting paid to ride her Appaloosa mare and take ski lessons at Bridger Bowl. While she closed the horse trailer I stared into the thunderstorm, finding that it matched my mood. Then the sun broke low from under the edge of the thunderhead, igniting a row of pale limestone hogbacks. They stood like a saw blade buried in the mountainside, glowing with light. A silver sheet of hail draped the canyon, leaving the dark emerald of freshly washed meadows in its wake. The sun grew stronger and a double rainbow scribed a graceful arc over the Gallatin River, its arms stretching deep into the wilderness on both sides.

As we headed down the canyon into the retreating storm, I thought again about the "bad jobs" discussion. While some might consider removing old fish heads from fire rings a pretty nasty task, packing trash that day felt like public service. As the Gallatin Canyon rainbow intensified I felt some kind of peace with Nancy, though we were to remain circumspect with each other for the rest of our years as colleagues. On that afternoon we shared a gratitude for having spent the day outdoors doing work that seemed worthwhile. For the moment, it was enough.

7

AT THE MAIN BOULDER RANGER STATION five of us donned fireproof pants, bright yellow Nomex shirts and metal hardhats for a five-minute helicopter ride. Our destination was Mt. Rae, a 9,237-foot peak on the northern boundary of the Absaroka-Beartooth Wilderness. The helicopter arrived, with two geologists who worked for one of the country's largest minerals companies. The helicopter could take three at a time, and I was part of the first group to fly to the summit.

The green composition roof of the Main Boulder ranger station quickly shrank to postage-stamp size, while directly in front of us loomed Mt. Rae with its bare ridge of ragged krummholz and scree. A remnant of snow hung off the mountain's east shoulder like a feather boa. The pilot set the ship gently onto a saddle four thousand feet above the ranger station and we sidestepped away, hunched over at the waist as if ducking under a turnstile. Before I stood up, the helicopter had lifted off again.

I peeled off my Nomex, required for agency employees in case the helicopter crashed, while we waited for the rest of the party. We introduced ourselves, exploration geologists and national forest officials, there to represent different points of view. The field season of 1983 would be the last before the Wilderness Act turned twenty years old, and according to the law, the last opportunity for private interests to stake claims for hard-rock minerals within the boundaries of designated wilderness. The mineral company was looking for platinum-group minerals, and preparing to assay surface rocks. They had requested access to several high-mountain sites by helicopter and the Forest Service granted it, with the proviso that we be invited along to approve the landing zones.

I was there to offer advice on issues relating to wilderness character and its preservation, as if an open-pit mine could be made compatible with such values. The forest hydrologist was along, and the local district ranger, who would approve or nix the proposed helipads based on our discussion.

Introductions made, light chit-chat was attempted and soon abandoned. The geologists were used to riding in helicopters, whereas I had never been in one before. Regardless of our levels of experience, none of us could keep from looking around in wonder at how fast we had reached the heights of Mt. Rae. The Crazy Mountains stretched across the northern skyline and the prairie of the upper Yellowstone River Basin draped folds of tan and fading green toward the eastern horizon. Scree dropped toward glacier-carved canyons at our feet where the Boulder River wound through pastures and farms, north toward the town of Big Timber. When we turned to face the wind and scan to the south, a sea of peaks tumbled toward us like cresting waves.

Stan was the mineral company's lead geologist. Roughly my age, his curly brown hair held the first traces of gray and his face was wrinkled from years of working under the sun. I immediately liked him, a composite of all the youngish, affable geologists I had known and the men from undergraduate classes with whom I studied and drank beer when I was an aspiring geologist myself. I spoke his language, and nodded with understanding as he gave an overview of the geologic terrane we were about to traverse.

"Chrome deposits are rare," he said. "Stillwater chromites represent 80 percent of chromium reserves in the Western Hemisphere."

He didn't have to state what was obvious to us all, that under the 1872 mining law that was still in effect over a century later, and with deposits of important strategic minerals needed to make high-grade steel, the Forest Service would have little influence on the development of a mine other than to suggest mitigation. Stream banks would be protected during road construction and measures to contain tailings and wastewater would be called for, but the prospect of a major development on the border of the wilderness was without question. Our field trip that day would result in landing zones for exploration having as little permanent impact as possible, but this seemed a minor concession compared to the extent of what was to come. Or not, perhaps; it all depended on the fluctuating value of the minerals.

We gazed across the Main Boulder to Chrome Mountain where a mine that dated from a World War II minerals rush could be seen. After the war demand for chrome fell and the mines, roads, and buildings were abandoned. Chrome, Iron, and Picket Pin Mountains, where switchback roads and diggings from the past were clearly visible, lay well north of the wilderness boundary, with proven deposits and a partially repairable infrastructure. A new mine to the west, possibly within the wilderness, would have much more impact than reopening the existing ones. But those claims were already staked and Stan's company was interested in more than chrome. Under the Beartooth Mountains lay the Stillwater Complex, a geologic oddity of layered igneous rock so singular it was featured in mineralogy textbooks. The only other such deposit on earth was found in Greenland.

The Stillwater Complex is a layered intrusion thirty miles long and 2.7 billion years old. The gneiss into which the magma was intruded is even older. More intrusions followed, along with intense metamorphism, faulting, and folding, making a jumble of the layered sequence and tilting it to nearly vertical in places. All of this happened long before the Paleozoic era when life on earth began. The exposed thickness of the complex is around eighteen thousand feet and it is estimated that as much as fifteen thousand feet was eroded away before the first Cambrian sediments were deposited on top. Inconceivable violence in an inconceivably distant past.

If the pre-Cambrian history isn't a story to enchant the imagination, there is more.

The Stillwater Complex comprises three distinct zones. At the base is a relatively thin layer of gabbro, norite, and pyroxenite. The ultramafic zones (dense with iron and magnesium, making the rock very dark) are composed of a complex sequence of rocks, some of which are rare enough to receive only passing mention in petrology texts: chromitite, harzburgite, bronzite. The names, while unfamiliar on the tongue, speak of great antiquity and a long and turbulent past, the way a story might begin with *long ago and far away*. When Stan unfolded a geologic map of the area we would hike, from the top of Mt. Rae back down into the Boulder River valley, this long-remembered story came to life again.

The helicopter skimmed the ridge, bearing the last of our group. The chop-chop-chop of long rotor blades faded into the distance, leaving us alone on the mountain in a gusting wind, with the day's hike ahead.

I fell into stride with Stan and we were quickly ahead of the others, which gave us time to probe the margins of a talus slope. He picked up a common-looking gray rock.

"Norite," he said, and handed it to me.

I had only held this kind of rock as a hand specimen in petrology lab.

"It's such a light color for an ultramafic." I turned the rock over in my hand, wondering at the unimaginable span of time that had brought it from a molten state, miles under the surface of the earth, to the top of a mountain in Montana.

Stan glanced at me with a question on his face until I told him I had a geology degree, though I was quick to point out it had been years. But he was glad to have a hiking companion who knew what he was talking about.

"This norite has minute quantities of chrome. Some of what we'll sample, to see how disseminated it is."

By reflex I grasped at my shirt collar, feeling for the hand lens I had not carried in years. Stan lent me his.

As the others caught up we shifted our conversation from norite to landing zones. We found an acceptable location for a large helicopter, one requiring no tree removal. Red flagging recorded our decision, and we moved on, Stan and I taking the lead. Our route included open talus, where he could assess the rocks and I could stop and stare across the Boulder River valley into the wild country beyond. I spoke his language; could he speak mine? In his thirties, past the age when most eager young geologists had abandoned the long grueling days of field work to become managers and lobbyists, Stan wore Carhartts rubbed smooth along the hip where his compass and rock hammer hung. Perhaps, like me, he was captivated by high country.

Maybe he would understand if I exclaimed about the alpine flowers or the distant view, the wilderness that inspired me. He was as fascinated by the rocks as I was, but did he brood over what might happen to the mountains in case of a major discovery? If he found chrome, it would probably mean a bonus in his paycheck. I could have worn his shoes once, but for circumstances and choices. Lacking a mentor or the discipline required, I abandoned geology for another field of study, but I continued to find joy in examining and wondering over rocks, alone in the mountains with my own compass and hammer. Now I was another sort of professional. My job was to protect the wilderness from this pleasant, friendly geologist doing the job that might have been mine.

Landing zones determined, we dropped into a forest of dog hair lodgepole pine in a dry gulch leading to the Boulder River. We spread out single file, in the quiet of our own thoughts. I paused to pick up a shred of faded survey flagging, probably left by a hunter the year before.

Steve, the forest hydrologist, asked with a smile, "So, are you a no-trace camper?" His voice carried a hint of derision.

"Something wrong with that?"

I felt my anger rise as I remembered him asking if I was a bra-burner. Why was I being made fun of? Was he trying to make me feel foolish for picking up a scrap of litter on the trail when the work we were doing might lead to a huge mine in what was then pristine backcountry? I had to admit it did seem silly in that context.

Stan had only glanced over his shoulder as I bent toward the flagging, probably wondering if I had found an interesting rock. He, whose employer was in the business of tearing mountains apart for chrome, did not reproach me. Maybe I had earned his respect by being able to match his pace and conversation. A respect I could not seem to earn from my coworkers.

Why did I abandon the study of geology, a field that once excited me? For one thing, I discovered that my bachelor's degree was not the ticket to a profession; instead it was the first ticket punched in a profession that required a PhD. And although I wanted to be afield, I did not want to work for a mining company. Such work struck me as pedestrian; I set my sights on high-minded research, the noble pursuit of science. But even science required a penance of drudgery. A summer job with the US Geological Survey had shown me that for every week spent banging on rocks in the mountains, I had to spend two in a windowless lab. The arm-waving zeal of undergraduates, discussing plate tectonics as if it were a theory we made up ourselves, dissolved into the conventions of scientific writing and uninspired talks at conferences.

What waited, if I continued to pursue science, was mostly boredom. What I wanted, if I were honest, was someone to tell me stories, the way Stan was doing now. How the rocks were formed, where they came from. How the world I knew came to be. I would have been as content with the story of Turtle Island as with the fantastic tales of sea-floor spreading and continental drift. The grain of sand that Turtle brought from the bottom of the sea, from which the creator fashioned North America, arrived courtesy of a convergent plate margin. I had just held the evidence, a fragment of norite. Myth or science, it was the same lovely story.

Geology had been my story, but it did not offer a career. My professors must have seen it in the way I looked beyond the rocks. My view of landscapes included plants and scenery and wildlife; my focus was distant and diffused. Derision was their way of discouraging me from a career that did not fit. I applied to graduate school, inspired by Don's sister Harriet. With her degree in landscape architecture, she was part of a backcountry research project for the Forest Service's Northeast Experiment Station. I had never heard of landscape architecture as a field of study, but being paid to hike sounded like my kind of work.

Following Stan down Mt. Rae made me wistful for the time when I listened to stories of the earth. I had gazed at the specimen of norite, surprised by how much I remembered of an igneous petrology class ten years before. I imagined the depths at which the rock formed, the processes by which this layer from the bottom of the earth's crust came to perch at ten thousand feet on a mountaintop. But the specks of valuable chrome in its matrix would never cause my pulse to quicken.

My ease at talking rocks with Stan jarred against the foreign sound of Forest Service lingo. Ugly and unimaginative acronyms like "LZ" for landing zone had replaced the musical and tantalizing names of minerals. More than arcane scientific jargon, the technical terms were passwords that admitted me into a society, like the hand lens that once hung around my neck.

With Stan on Mt. Rae I stepped back into the comfortable fold of the club. We walked under the broad Montana sky telling stories, waving our arms, remembering an old spark of excitement, the newfound thrill of talking rocks. It didn't matter that I was female and he was male. It didn't matter that I was there to preserve the mountain scenery and some quality of wilderness and he was there to find what could only be taken by destroying them.

The attention of the mining company eventually focused on the East Boulder River, where claims were staked. Construction commenced in the late 1990s after years of assay, testing, and planning, and commercial production began in 2002. The metals used in your car's catalytic converter might have come from the Stillwater Complex. Your personal computer's hard disk, video recorder, or MP3 player may contain platinum from the mines in the Beartooth Mountains.

The East Boulder Mine and tailings ponds occupy a little more than an acre of the surface, as most of the mine is underground. In its decade of operation, the mine has produced platinum-group minerals, though fluctuations in market, the inherent inefficiencies of ore recovery in a mine whose minerals are disseminated, and production costs have left it operating below capacity. The company is lately diversifying into recycling of the minerals it once dug out of the earth.

The day I hiked down the east slope of Mt. Rae was personally memorable for a number of reasons: I had survived my first ride in a helicopter, relieved to know we would be hiking down the mountain instead of flying back. I had seen the view from Mt. Rae, a grunt bushwhack that I would not have done on foot. But mostly, I remember Stan. He reminded me of my years as an undergrad, the girl being allowed for a little while into the club. I was an insider then, in a way that I had never been since.

Those memories seeped to the surface after that trip to Mt. Rae, and I have pondered them often. The geology I held in common with Stan, a stranger whom I would never see again, created a brief bond that ran deeper than the utilitarian brand of conservation I shared with my colleagues in the Forest Service. With Stan I felt accepted, while with Steve the hydrologist, I did not. But Steve was a pleasant and gentle soul, one who kept his cards so close to his chest (out of self-protection, I later surmised) that it was impossible to know what he really thought. He reminded me of Nancy in this regard. I took his comments about bra-burning and no-trace camping as insults, but it is possible they were not meant that way. I had become primed, expecting insults, and I found that what one expected, one received.

Lost among the rocks, 1983.

8

EMULATING SWEET, COMPLIANT NANCY was an elusive goal for me, though I sometimes wished for such magic. When I asked her boss, the Bozeman District ranger, to talk about the skills needed for a position like hers, he shrugged and said, "Just smile and be pleasant."

I was so intensely focused on my work it was hard to remember to smile, to sit back and take a break from an urgent task while I listened to someone's elk hunting tale. I forgot to ask my coworkers about themselves, since I didn't have time to wait for much of an answer. Most of the people I worked with seemed the same way—busy, preoccupied. We never meant to be brusque.

In 1985, a new receptionist brought a measure of civility and grace to the office. Edie had a smile for everyone and the way she asked questions showed her genuine interest in what others had to say. She organized a party for the forest ladies, as she called us. Edie and her husband Sam were members of the Salish-Kootenay Confederation, and as I passed the open garage door leading into their living room, a large poster glowered from inside: *Custer had it coming.*

I was the lone professional at Edie's party, among typists and accounting techs and mail clerks whom I had barely gotten to know at the office. One of them, whose insistence on retyping my purchase orders drove me nearly to despair, was hardly recognizable as she kicked back on the sofa with a glass of wine, her face ignited by laughter. Seeing her that way made me wonder how it felt to put on the dour purchasing-agent mask each workday. What masks did I wear to the job? I felt as though I still wore them as Edie passed the cookies, for I was shy and uncomfortable around these women and couldn't imagine what I might have to say that would interest them. It was more interesting to listen.

I listened with particular intensity to Annette, the woman who processed special-use permits for summer homes and backcountry outfitters.

In her early sixties at the time, she was large-bosomed and heavyset and would have been gray except for the jet-black dye in her hair. The clerks who worked with her considered her a formidable battle-ax and I had no reason to doubt them. She sighed often at her desk, grumped at anyone who stopped by with a question, and kept her face knitted into a perpetual frown as she stared at her computer screen. But that night she told stories of when she and her long-dead husband were young and living in Wisdom, a tiny berg in the Bighole River valley. They had a traveling swing band and she played saxophone. I never saw her the same way after that night, even though she brought the same resentful mask to work. She longed to retire but couldn't afford to. She cared about her looks as evidenced by her weekly hair appointments and the handful of neat sheaths and dresses she exchanged not quite often enough to keep you from noticing that she had only a few. Feared by her subordinates and dismissed by her bosses, Annette concealed that younger incarnation buried deep within her, the vivacious woman who played dance music with her husband and their friends. I felt I shared a secret of hers, knowing a little of her past. Until I left Montana, I greeted her as if she was still the young Annette, who might have spent the previous weekend traveling all over Montana to play the tenor sax.

I retained a warm feeling for the women at Edie's party but I never ate cookies with them again. Sam got a job with the Flathead tribe and he and Edie went home. They were a breath of fresh air for a couple of years, one that spoke well for "diversity"—not because they were American Indian but because Sam was a civil engineer who understood wildlife migration corridors and scenery, and Edie was an elegant, friendly, charming lady who made the most of her job as a receptionist. They left a vacuum behind, and in their wake I learned that others would soon be leaving as well.

Around the time Edie and Sam left the forest I was presented my "five-year pin" for having worked as a permanent full-time employee since 1980. While the forest supervisor grinned and shook my hand and the coffee crowd applauded, I ducked my head. Five years had slipped by and I had yet to acknowledge that I had chosen a career. The Forest Service appealed because I loved forests, but I had no love for government bureaucracy, arcane lingo, and tongue-twisting acronyms, and I had no desire to move onward and upward within the agency. Yet the longer I stayed the more I loved the forest and it occurred to me that loyalty to place, a relationship with the land, were more important than moving on to further one's career.

"No higher calling," Ross told me, "than to be a good steward of public land."

"Public land is the great equalizer," Joe said, with his usual fierce conviction. "It's what makes us different from countries where the aristocracy has all the land and nobody else can go there."

Both Ross and Joe grew up in rural working-class areas in upstate New York and Pennsylvania, where they spent their youth hunting and fishing. In those days youngsters could freely trespass on neighbors' private land, neighbors who were glad to have fewer white-tail deer raiding their orchards. But the neighbors grew old, sold their property, and moved away. Boys of the next generation had nowhere to go. Having witnessed the transformation of their favorite haunts, Joe and Ross attended forestry school and headed west to the vast national forests of the Rocky Mountains, just as Gifford Pinchot's first foresters had done at the turn of the twentieth century. They bore the torch that Pinchot passed with pride, and did their parts to manage the national forests with his enlightened utilitarian attitude in mind: *Where conflicting interests must be reconciled, the question shall always be answered from the standpoint of the greatest good for the greatest number in the long run.*

Unlike some of their peers, neither of them sought power or prestige, nor promotion that would require them to move from the place where they had settled and raised their children. They represented "amenity" resources that carried "soft targets" which could easily be ignored without reprimand from above: recreation, wilderness, scenic quality. They had to stay on their toes to keep from being manipulated by other staff whose primary motivation seemed to be winning an argument and having their way. The prevailing Forest Service culture of the time allowed for the timber staff to be an advocate for industry, the minerals staff to promote mining and energy leasing, and the range staff to maximize the number of cow-calf pairs allowed on each grazing allotment. It was part of the concept of greatest good—all those jobs and the economic prosperity they created. Managing the forest for ecological purposes alone made no sense in this context. Unlike commodities such as timber, the benefits of amenity resources couldn't be described in terms of widgets produced or economic value (in recent decades this has changed dramatically and the economic impact of public wild lands is increasingly well documented). Thus a perpetual disconnect existed between commodity and amenity resources that manifested in every meeting or conversation about a proposed road or timber sale.

Ross taking a break along the Cherry Creek Trail, 1984.

They had their own disagreements as well, Joe playing John Muir to Ross's Gifford Pinchot, but they remained cordial colleagues and good friends. Representing underdog resources within the forest staff, they supported one another and presented a formidable team.

When Joe retired and I replaced him, I was tested. One day the timber staff came into my office to ask about a specialist report in which I had expressed concern about another timber sale planned for Bozeman Creek, which had recently been cut, or "harvested," to use agency lingo—as if the Forest Service had planted those trees like a crop. The number of clearcuts, along with their size, shape (square), and distribution, would detract from the scenery, I said. Townspeople looked out their windows to the canyon of Bozeman Creek, and it was impossible to make any additional cuts look natural.

"Which units in particular?" he asked.

Without a map to point to, I tried to describe the largest clearcut near the end of a proposed road.

"Are you talking about the clearcut or the unit?"

I stared. Weren't they the same thing? I was too embarrassed to ask him such a basic question and demonstrate my ignorance.

"Both," I said.

Our circular discussion continued until I simply stated that I didn't want to see another diaper line. With a smirk that broadened into a genuine smile, he nodded. We understood each other at last.

I was determined to overcome my discomfort, and that of others with me, by producing outstanding work. But it wasn't a detailed and beautifully rendered site design for a trailhead parking lot that mattered—a different kind of excellence earned favor in the Forest Service, particularly for women. *Smile and be pleasant.* I could render trailhead plans forever, carefully placing wide-radius curves so people driving horse trailers wouldn't have to back up, but what ended up being constructed never varied—a square patch of bare earth bulldozed into the sagebrush. The engineer I worked with, when he saw my drawings, would screw up his face in misery and whine. "Why does there always have to be a turn-around?"

I explained the reasoning behind the angled parking slots and sixty-foot radius curves, knowing the backhoe driver would never see my site plan. One square patch after another appeared in the sage and people seemed to figure out how to park their vehicles to everyone's satisfaction. Despite the futility of doing so, I continued to do my best.

The work came more easily when I worked on projects for which I had a natural attraction. The energy I found in wilderness work was enough for me to feel at times as if I had found my niche in the Forest Service. I initiated the Gallatin National Forest's first systematic inventory of backcountry campsite conditions and the first school-based program of wilderness education, modeled on the excellent example provided by the adjacent Custer National Forest. My enthusiasm blinded me to an obvious circumstance, that the more the wilderness education program was seen as my initiative, the less others had a stake in it. Resistance came in many forms, from a sudden lack of funds to produce trailhead information signs to declarations by rangers that they didn't want the wilderness educator I had hired to show up on "their" districts.

"He's not going to your district," I said. "He's going to the schools in town."

Evidently the local schools were included within the fiefdoms of rangers, for soon the educator was restricted to the Bozeman area while the districts had their own employees give presentations to the schools, talks whose content could be controlled by the ranger. In my mind a forest-wide program provided consistency and helped the ranger districts by performing a task they would not be asked to do with their limited funds.

In their minds, I was another rock thrown into their paths by the supervisor's office. I didn't understand how deeply the district rangers wanted to run their own show. Answerable to some degree to the forest supervisor, often after a dressing down, they would continue their behavior in more subtle and inconspicuous ways. It was a cat and mouse game as old as the Forest Service, recorded by one of the first forest rangers who reported in his journal, "Saw the supervisor four times this year. He saw me twice."

The ranger's chair attracted willful people who liked to make decisions. Then along came legislation that resulted in more than 40 percent of the Gallatin National Forest becoming Congressionally designated as part of the Absaroka-Beartooth and Lee Metcalf Wildernesses. Some rangers saw this development as tying their hands, and in a part of the country that still held vast tracts of backcountry, they thought there was already plenty of wilderness. Losing control over what could be done within their district boundaries, they were now confronted with an upstart in the SO who didn't think they were doing enough.

"These guys are hostile to the very idea of wilderness," I complained.

"She's trying to give direction to my employees," they countered.

I didn't want to see the wilderness program sputter to a halt when I left, and I didn't want to isolate myself as some of my colleagues had done through their insistence that they be listened to. Their frustration was easy to understand, especially with Sara, the beleaguered biologist whose input was challenged at every step. She cited peer-reviewed research as well as her own carefully documented monitoring to make her arguments while the timber planners got by with simple declarations of "professional opinion," opinion which, though often flawed, prevailed. "Why even keep a biologist on the staff," she fumed. Why keep any of the Ologists who were paid to provide their professional opinions and help management make better decisions? It must have been more fun, and certainly more in keeping with the wild-west origins of the USDA Forest Service Region One, to ignore specialist input and end up in appeals or in court where environmentalists could take the blame for obstructing progress.

Smart and thoughtful people worked for both the Forest Service and environmental groups. On the subject of wild land management I thought we should be allies. I hosted potlucks to which I invited them all—Ross and Sara and environmental advocates. I hoped these chances to develop personal relationships would overcome the discomfort people felt for one another. Whether this happened or not I cannot say, but anyone attending

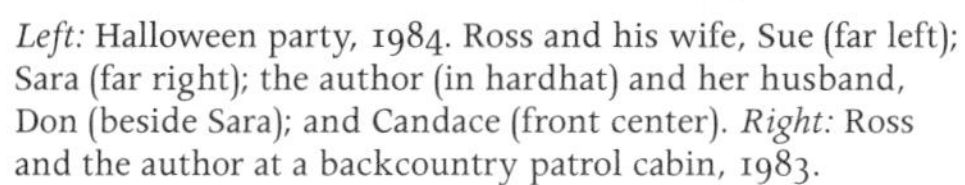

Left: Halloween party, 1984. Ross and his wife, Sue (far left); Sara (far right); the author (in hardhat) and her husband, Don (beside Sara); and Candace (front center). *Right:* Ross and the author at a backcountry patrol cabin, 1983.

a party of mine knew they would likely have to talk with someone they otherwise would not have known. Good sports all, they kept coming.

Though I was an advocate for wild land I held no disdain for the mission of the Forest Service. The Multiple-Use Sustained-Yield Act of 1960 directed the Forest Service to develop and manage renewable resources, but it did not say that every acre should be managed for every possible use—which was the interpretation I frequently encountered among the timber staff. The law provided for maintenance of the land's productivity "with consideration being given to the relative values of the various resources, and not necessarily the combination of uses that will give the greatest dollar return or the greatest unit output." And also, this: "The establishment and maintenance of areas of wilderness are consistent with the purposes and provisions of this Act."

I saw nothing to disagree with in the Act's refreshingly succinct two pages. But multiple-use was invoked as the clinching argument for building roads in grizzly bear habitat, converting hiking trails to three-wheeler routes, and cutting timber in municipal watersheds.

Through times of frustration and self-doubt I knew I could rely on Ross, always ready to head for the field and take a look at anything that needed our appraisal, from a campground to a clearcut. We spent a day together in a driving rain at Lava Lake in the Spanish Peaks, where he gamely helped survey the condition of popular campsites. His makeshift slicker was one of the garbage bags we hadn't filled. On another occasion we drove up the potholed road that led to Hyalite Reservoir, where he argued—no, shouted—with the forest engineer about whether or not the roadway should be paved. It was the usual battle between facts that could be stated quantitatively and the no-less-real sense of place that had yet to make its way into Forest Service parlance. The engineer had the facts, as well as promised funding from the regional office, on his side: the road would have to be improved anyway since the reservoir was scheduled for reconstruction that would require heavy equipment. People wanted it plowed in winter, not possible on rutted gravel. Dust and runoff were dumping directly into the creek.

"We've never had any trouble keeping that road plowed if you get on it right away," Ross countered. "And the whole feel of the place would change. A paved road encourages people to drive too fast."

The engineer blew a gust of air through his nose. Paving was the answer, end of discussion.

"God damned narrow-minded engineer," Ross muttered later. We both laughed, me mostly out of relief that I wasn't the only one who was ignored and put in my place when I dared to disagree with someone who had made up his mind. Not long after I arrived in Bozeman the same engineer had come into my office to deliver a lecture on the principles of road design. I listened to his monologue with as much patience as I could muster before mentioning that I had a degree in a field that required some knowledge of road design, and there was more to consider than gradient and drainage. I started to pose questions about the user's experience and he stomped out the door, shaking his head.

As it happened, Hyalite Creek road was paved a few years later, and the first weekend it was open a high school kid took a corner too fast, rolled his truck, and died.

Though in his late forties, a few pounds overweight and suffering from sciatic nerve impingement, Ross was willing to give backpacking a try. I gathered that he had not donned a backpack in some time as we planned our trip of three days into the Hilgard Basin, part of the newly designated Lee Metcalf Wilderness. Bill, the area's single wilderness ranger, and the only other person from the ranger district willing to go, Rae Ellen—on a year's appointment for recreation planning—joined us.

We hiked seven miles up Sentinel Creek until the trail split at the base of Expedition Pass. The southern branch of the trail led over a divide into the Hilgard Basin, climbing to a gap along a spur ridge where pockets of bare soil were scratched into the talus by mountain goats making their beds. The sky arched between horizons without a hint of cloud, its margins serrated by jagged rock. It was mid-August and the green-draped basin held an edge of bronze and gold, hints of autumn in the turf of alpine rush. Brittle seedheads of the year's wildflowers rattled in the breeze while snow banks from the previous winter remained tucked into steep slopes shadowed by north-facing walls of bedrock.

It was the chance to see a place like this for the first time that made my heart swell with delight and gratitude for having found the perfect profession. Don and I filled our weekends with hikes and overnight camping trips, as we would have done regardless of where we worked. With spectacular high country as part of my workplace, I felt proud of the Forest Service and pleased to be a part of it. Dwarfed by the presence of magnificent mountains were all the trolls and gremlins waiting at the office, nipping at each other's heels. Children bickering in the sandbox while the real world unfurled as it always had, with sublime beauty.

We made camp near Expedition Lake, taking care to pitch our tents well away from the water's edge. Echo Peak dominated the view of the mountain crest, one of four summits in the Taylor-Hilgard Unit of the Lee Metcalf Wilderness that exceeded eleven thousand feet. Long ridges north and south of the summit culminated in a faceted peak that looked like a great cut jewel, roughly pyramidal and striped with shadows and snowfields. Echo was the crown of the rockscape surrounding us, standing far above the unnamed intermediate peaks that by themselves formed an impressive range. It was hard to take my gaze away from that distinctive mountain until the last light of evening left it.

Ross must have rummaged in his basement for camp equipment, most of which looked like remnants of his son's Boy Scout days, or perhaps his own. His backpack was a faded external frame that might have fit his petite wife, but Ross was imperviousness to discomfort when his will to be outdoors prevailed. His hands felt no cold in ice water, his back no lumps from the ground on which he slept.

Echo Peak glowed like an ember in the first light of morning. The sun, only a few degrees above the horizon, already felt warm. The sound of camp stoves broke the silence like a hangar full of tiny jet engines, so

Historic outfitter camp at Expedition Lake with Echo Peak in the distance, 1950s (USFS photo).

loud, especially my old Svea, that you had to raise your voice to be heard. Once the water for coffee and oatmeal had boiled, the stoves fell silent and a blessed quiet descended. Ross was still fiddling with his Sterno stove, which consisted of a tin of wax surrounded by a flimsy set of hinged plates meant to hold a cook pot. At least the thing was quiet, with its blue flame weakly trying to reach the base of the pot. The rest of us, more pained to watch his efforts than he was, had extra hot water and insisted he use it.

After breakfast we conferred over which of the many lake basins to visit, eager to see as much of what Ross called the *Hil-de-gards* as possible during the middle day of our three-day trip. Bill caught me eyeing Echo's north ridge.

"It's an easy climb," he said. "A scramble, really."

"You've done it."

He nodded and I looked around at our group to gauge their interest. Rae Ellen raised her eyebrows, a gesture I took for enthusiasm. Ross stared at Echo Peak.

"A pretty peak," Bill said.

Pretty. That wasn't it at all. Such a word struck me as trivial as I beheld the power and beauty of that mountain, but I kept my opinion to myself.

"I would love to make it up that thing," Ross said.

We packed lunch and told each other we had no mandatory destination, we would simply hike in the general direction of Echo until we found a great viewpoint or felt like turning back. I was elected route-finder.

I aimed for the north ridge, where bedrock ribs softened into wide soft cups of sedge and rush. Shreds of mountain goat fleece fluttered from the branches of stiff and shrubby subalpine firs, showing the way to a faint track angling up the slope toward the crest of the Madison Range. As we gained elevation the Hilgard Basin spread below, a patchwork of sparkling lakes, frost-heave hummocks, and bands of whitebark pine. To the north Expedition Pass was a talus-mantled col.

The goat trail led us to the divide a few hundred yards south of Expedition Pass. The Hilgard Basin was lush compared to the west slope of the range, a desolate tumble of talus and spires of shattered bedrock dotted by a few barren-looking lakes. The Madison River valley spread like a straw mat beyond the great alluvial fans at the foot of the mountains. We took in the view in silence until Ross pointed and said, "Would you look at that."

Echo Lake lay below, opaque and milky green from suspended sediment flushed from the foot of a rock glacier. Above its surface soared two Bald Eagles, gaining altitude as they traced the edges of the lake. Perhaps if they attracted eagles, those lakes may not be as barren as they looked. We watched the eagle pair climb until they found a stream of wind, still below eye level, and tilted their wings toward the red and buff-striped slopes of the Taylor Peaks.

Frost and time had disintegrated the gneiss into crumbling saprolite that crunched like beach sand underfoot. The divide was gentle for a quarter mile while the north ridge of Echo Peak loomed ahead, an impenetrable fortress.

"It's easier than it looks from here," Bill told us.

He was right, for as we reached the base of the steep north ridge we could see the well-beaten trail of mountain goats and climbers. The trail corkscrewed its way around blocks of amphibolite the size of my car. I was glad the outcrops truncated our view of the exposed slopes below. It felt like climbing a stone staircase, one step at a time, easy steps with plenty to hold onto.

Just as we began to relax the ridge became steeper and the stone steps farther apart. I started using my hands to help haul myself up. The exposure off the east side loomed closer.

"This is starting to get a little hairy," Ross ventured.

"If it gets hairy, I'm not going," I said.

Since I still felt comfortable, with my lifelong vertigo when faced with a long drop at my toes, he followed along, confident that I would chicken out before he did. By now Bill was far in front of us, while I led Ross and Rae Ellen up the easiest and most protected route I could find. We went slowly, carefully, all of us wondering if some scary crux move would keep us from our goal. But the ridge widened and the way became obvious and easy. We walked out onto a wide platform, the summit of Echo.

We stood beside the brass monument left by the Geologic Survey, a benchmark named *Roof* where lichen-encrusted bedrock and alpine tundra formed a kind of sod roof over the gently sloping summit. Hilgard Peak tugged at our gaze with its pair of dark metamorphic towers jabbing at the sky.

Mountains in three states etched the horizon. The Henry's Lake Mountains on the Idaho border rose behind the shoulder of Hilgard Peak. Westward, the banded face of the Centennials cut the horizon above Red Rock Lakes National Wildlife Refuge. A long ridge of forest and high prairie west of the Madison River formed the crest of the Gravelly Range; beyond it the Snowcrest Mountains faded into the same blue as the sky. Shedhorn Mountain stood to the north, and behind it the Spanish Peaks. Sacajawea, the highest point in the Bridger Range north of Bozeman, hovered like a ghost peak in the distance between two closer summits. The Crazies to the far northeast were a pale silhouette of peaks jutting into the prairie. More ranges of mountains stood before them: the Gallatin Range marching into Yellowstone Park, the Absarokas following beyond. Farther still a high plateau, barely visible: the Beartooth. In the relative foreground, the canyon of Sentinel Creek and the trail we had hiked the day before was lost in folds of forest, with only a crease of shadow to show where the creek flowed into Beaver Creek and Beaver Creek into the Madison River. From Echo Peak we could skim the wide expanse of Hebgen Lake, moving upstream until the Madison River disappeared into Yellowstone National Park. The lodgepole pine forest of the Madison Plateau was broken by a single gash, the canyon where the Firehole and Gibbon Rivers met to form the river's headwaters. To the southeast, snow still clung to Coffin Mountain on the Continental Divide. In the shimmering distance, hovering like a bank of clouds, stood the Teton Range.

The author on Echo Peak, Lee Metcalf Wilderness, 1984.

Dizzy, I sat for a while and stared at the mountain ranges surrounding Echo Peak. I dug under a rock pile to find the worn pages of a summit register where others had scribbled their exclamations. The usual "wow" and "we made it!" statements were mixed with heartfelt and eloquent prayers to the gods of mountains. I found a number of sketches in the register, as if the artist was unable to believe the view unless it was reproduced on paper. A surprising number of people wrote brief but moving poems. Each had stood on these summit rocks astounded by what they saw, from the panorama of ranges on all horizons to the way the dry straw of alpine grass stood out against dark lichens in the waning light of a late summer afternoon. I wanted to add to this long collective poem, to record my visit with more than slack-jawed staring, but I managed only a line or two, a proto-poem that had no beginning and no end:

Below our feet
Half the West falls away.

After expressing his deep satisfaction, Ross declared it to be nap time and sprawled between boulders on a bed of alpine turf. The others took his cue while I remained seated with knees bent, bootless toes cooled by the mountain breeze, forearms wrapping my shins. From my perch it was easy to see the interdependencies of mountains and valleys, the way the public wild lands and human settlements wove together to form a landscape full of promise, where decisions made decades ago did not constrain our options. The human communities depended on these wild mountains for their context, as scenic backdrops and places for inspiration, and mostly, to nurture their spirits. The wilderness depended on communities of wise and far-thinking individuals, for its fate would always be decided by those who lived here.

In the summit register's poetry the mountain spoke through its human visitors, asking only that we take a moment to remember what high country had always inspired in our ancestors—wonder, rapture, awe—and pass these traits to our children. Poets must have joined the cartographers when the Hilgard Basin's early maps were drawn. Some of the names described what could be seen from high above, lakes called Crag and Talus and Little Pine. Others described how it felt to be there: Comet, Sunset, Thunderbolt, Expedition, and Blue Paradise.

9

WHILE THE MEMORY OF A MAN BEING EATEN by a grizzly bear faded with the years, my unrelenting apprehension kept me north of occupied habitat whenever I hiked alone. One of the places I came to know best was the Spanish Peaks, at the northern edge of the Gallatin Range and a few miles south of Bozeman. When the area was included in the Lee Metcalf Wilderness it gave me an excuse to inventory baseline conditions along trails and popular campsites—at the time, the only human influences we could do very much about. But for one season in the mid-1980s I was glad to retreat from what we called "The Peaks" altogether. A young woman had disappeared while jogging on a trail near the Big Sky ski resort.

Bear attack leapt into everyone's mind, but we soon discovered that grizzly bears were not the only fearsome creatures in the forest.

Kari Swenson ran alone on forest paths surrounding the Big Sky Resort every afternoon, in training for the US Olympic biathlon team. When she failed to return from a jog around Ulerys Lakes, a pair of friends scoured her route, alarmed to see fresh bear tracks along the trail that Kari had taken. But she hadn't been attacked by a bear; the two men searched through the night and found her the next morning. Tied to a tree and attended by two armed guards.

Kari and one of her would-be rescuers were shot in the early morning encounter. The other friend fled. When sheriff's deputies arrived at the scene hours later, the men with the rifle were gone and Kari's friend Alan, shot in the face from close range, lay dead. They found Kari curled in a filthy sleeping bag and bleeding from a chest wound. From her hospital bed in Bozeman she told a harrowing tale.

A grizzled man in late middle-age accompanied by a youth with long, greasy hair had stepped in front of her on the trail and led her to their camp at gunpoint. As evening fell she drew her knees up and accepted

Along the divide between Spanish and Moonlight Creeks, Lee Metcalf Wilderness.

the sleeping bag they offered, for all she had against the mountain chill were skimpy jogging shorts and a tee shirt. Time passed and their words became more menacing. *We just want someone to talk to* became *Spend a few days with us.* She slowly learned their purpose—female company for the younger man.

Kari's description of her abductors rang some bells among the sheriff's deputies. Sounds like Dan and Don Nichols, someone said. As word about the fugitives spread, calls poured into the sheriff's office. Every father-son hiking team on every mountain trail in Montana matched their description. They'd been seen in Billings, Ennis, and the Cowboy Bar in Jackson Hole. But most likely they were still in the Spanish Peaks, keeping to the rough breaks and lonely ridges far from well-traveled trails.

Armed and extremely dangerous, the trailhead posters warned. Backcountry rangers worked in pairs and we kept our radios handy. Some of us were teamed with sheriff's deputies at roadblocks and trailheads to warn backpackers away while helicopters swept low overhead. The Nichols team soon acquired a nickname: the mountain men.

That such a title had been conferred upon these two dirt bags rankled Bozemanites. Until that moment the region's heritage as part of the 1820s fur trade had rested comfortably enough alongside our latter-day pride in local Olympic hopefuls. Our town was named for a mountain man, the trapper and explorer John Bozeman, and there was an annual canoe race on the Madison River named for Liver-Eatin' Johnson. Though coarse and ungoverned individuals, the early trappers' violent ways had long been rendered into benign, if not heroic, legend. I thought of them as various incarnations of the capable and honorable Dick Summers of A. B. Guthrie's novels. Now the mountain men of history faded into disreputable myth, and Summers was replaced by kidnappers, murderers.

Time split like the waters on either side of a divide: before and after the mountain men. Before, I had hiked alone in the Spanish Peaks, ankle-deep in mountain heather. I had rambled with joy over ribs of naked gneiss, its ribbons of melted and recrystallized black and gray punctuated by deep-red garnet thumbprints. After the mountain men, the heather withered and the rocks turned dark and foreboding. As refuge for armed renegades, these mountains could not shelter me.

Before, the people I encountered on hiking trails were part of a clan with nothing to fear from one other. Criminals did not backpack; they lurked in alleys and city parks. After, a distrustful reticence displaced the natural warmth people felt toward others on the trail. Every group of hikers I met had at least one large, intimidating dog, a pistol clearly displayed, and tight smiles that did not come easily. We asked each other as we passed, "Seen anything?" and when we shook our heads in reply we left each other with a few moments of relief.

Other than helping with trailhead patrols ("I'm sorry that you drove all the way from Illinois to hike this trail but I really can't recommend it . . .") I suspended my trips to the Spanish Peaks for the rest of the summer. Even in the distant Absaroka-Beartooth Wilderness, apprehension dogged my steps. One night I woke suddenly to the sound of branches snapping outside my tent. I raised my head and listened hard but all I could hear was the prattle of the creek and an intermittent wind in the trees. Overcast had moved in behind the setting near-full moon, and when I peeked out of the tent fly I saw only dense, inky darkness. Then came another snap—too close. Then a sound like scrambling footsteps—certain, definite, human. Someone was out there.

I felt around for something to use for a weapon and considered shouting for my partner, but his tent was pitched beside the creek where even if awake he probably wouldn't hear me. A shout would only alert the intruder to my presence, my femaleness, my fear. Sleeping bag wrapped around me like a shawl, I sat cross-legged with one hand clasped on a hiking boot until dawn began to seep through the spruces.

"Looks like you had a rough night," Phil said as he watched me stumbling around camp. He poured water into a bowl of instant oatmeal. "Bear anxiety?"

"I would have been relieved to know it was a bear. Didn't you hear all that scrabbling?"

Phil thought a moment before he revealed that he'd gotten up in the night to pee and without a flashlight had run straight into a tree. "I was trying to be quiet," he said.

August passed, September passed, and the sheriff's posse, a SWAT team from Billings, the National Guard's low-flying helicopters, and a horde of volunteers kept searching. Along the rugged crest of the Spanish Peaks, Don Nichols and his son left a cold trail of campsites and hastily emptied caches. They traveled on foot in terrain no horse or helicopter could penetrate, in mountains that no one knew better. The faces on the trailhead posters faded in the summer sun but they stayed vivid in my mind. The

Red Mountain, Madison County, Montana, not far from Dan and Don Nichols's last campsite.

elder man's eyes looked downward with a resignation that said he'd been there before, sitting for a prison mug shot. His son glanced upward and away from between long parted bangs with a sweet, shy smile, a photograph from his high school yearbook.

The searchers brought home stories of food caches, dugout hideaways, and turnip gardens they'd found in the Spanish Peaks. Hikers counted coup on them, returning from trips with scraps of abandoned gear. Cabin owners reported odd break-ins, the canned peaches missing while stereos and cash went undisturbed. An outfitter claimed to have seen them near his camp and boasted that he'd fed them without mentioning it to the sheriff. Already these mountain men had begun to go the way of their nineteenth-century namesakes, the stuff of legend, tomorrow's heroes.

"I can't believe they've got gardens up there," I said to one of the deputies.

"I've seen 'em," he said.

I raised a skeptical eyebrow. I could barely coax a crop of turnips from the ground in Bozeman before frost. How could these guys farm at nine thousand feet?

"Over by the Bear Trap," Bobby said. The Bear Trap, I knew from long experience by now, was the warm spot, nestled against the forests of the

Spanish Peaks but thousands of feet lower than the highest crags. It was possible that somewhere among the dark metamorphic boulders, abandoned gold prospects, and forests that fanned upward from the Madison River, Don and his nineteen-year-old son were holed up, harvesting their turnips and hiding from the law.

The low light of October raked through blond-cured grasses on the shoulders of the Spanish Peaks as the search for the mountain men narrowed to Bear Trap Canyon. By the middle of December the manhunt came to an end. The mountain men were camped in a draw west of the river and a rancher checking his cows spotted campfire smoke. It seemed unlike Don Nichols, who had slipped through the forest like a shadow for months, to become careless enough to camp within a mile of a road and let the smoke from his sputtering fire drift into the big Montana sky. But the weather had gathered early into one of the coldest and snowiest winters in years, so perhaps he had endured enough of hiding out, wet and hungry and barely alive. His son must have been fed up as well, particularly after the failed quest for female company and no prospect of another. Perhaps the smoke signal was a gesture of surrender.

The sheriff found the mountain men crouched under soaked tarps beside their smoky campfire. He must have wondered how to announce himself as he peered over the edge of an outcrop with a shotgun in his hand, knowing who hunkered there below. He settled for a standard greeting in rural Montana at that time of year.

"You boys seen any coyotes?"

For most of us the story of the mountain men settled into history. Kari Swenson had recovered, and though she missed the Olympics she was slowly regaining her strength. The following summer, Forest Service rangers hiked the Spanish Peaks again and rediscovered the art of friendly greetings on the trail. But the legend of Dan and Don did not die quietly, and I found myself in odd sympathy with them. While not excusing what he'd done, I pictured with sadness Don Nichols behind bars for the rest of his life, a wild creature in a cage and forever banished from the mountains he loved. Near the trail where Kari had been kidnapped stood a pine tree carved with these words of defiant claim: *Dan and Don Nichols live in these mountains.*

I was glad they no longer lived there. But I couldn't disagree with what Don had told the sheriff on his way to jail: the white man's world was a mess, and the hills offered freedom and escape. In short, he fled to the mountains for the same reasons I did. The fears, regrets, and paranoia that drove him deep into the backcountry were only a few shades darker than my own. We shared a love of place and despair over greed and materialism. I had only learned the game of fitting in better than he had. Or I was more willing to play.

Dan and Don may have lived in those mountains for a time, but their ways, like those of the original mountain men, belonged to an earlier era. It was no longer accepted practice to poach game all summer and leave caches in the wilderness and obtain a girlfriend through abduction. In an age when the wilderness itself was nearly gone, we all helped to perpetuate what was left of it by no longer living there. I lived as close to wild country as I could, and chose a signature rock and wildflower to make each range of mountains mine. A superficial gesture, but it tried to say the same thing that was carved into that pine tree. The mountains did not belong to me, but I to them.

On the first anniversary of the kidnapping, I camped beside my favorite alpine lake in the Spanish Peaks. That evening I climbed a spur ridge to the high divide where waters spilled south into the Madison River, north into the Gallatin. Pines bronzed by the setting sun cast long shadows down the slope. Rising trout broke the silver surface of the lake below, sending rings across the pale reflections of the sky. I paused at the place where one of the Nichols' food caches had been discovered. A pile of tumbled rocks, no more noteworthy than a fallen-down cairn or the abandoned scour of a mountain goat, marked the spot.

I sat beside the rubble of the cache and gazed across to Cedar Mountain, its solemn face blue with dusk. Between us rose the headwaters of the creeks where Dan and Don hid out, a network of traces that carried snowmelt to the Madison River. Ulerys Lakes lay obscured by trees. Glints of water gleamed dull pewter in the failing light, like shards of a broken mirror.

From the divide each branch of water was a dark crease in the forest, its rushing cascade rendered silent by distance. But the names of the tributaries repeated themselves in my mind, recalling events that took place among them the year before. The young man shot and left to die, the Olympic athlete bleeding in an old sleeping bag, unable to help her friend or herself. The sudden whop of a helicopter, flattening a field of wildflowers in its wash before it disappeared over the next ridge. The faces on the trailhead posters that had disappeared months before, now lingering like campfire smoke among the forests of Hammond, Jack, and Moonlight Creeks.

A chilly wind sent me back to camp. Traversing the flowered ramps between spines of stone, I found that mountain heather and garnet gneiss reassuringly cradled my steps. The Spanish Peaks were home again, but it was a different sort of home, a place where I no longer left the car keys in the ignition or the front door unlocked.

I'd nearly reached my tent when I spied a man walking along the lakeshore. His hair was long, like Dan's. Streaked with gray, like Don's. But now, on the far side of the divide that had split the world into Before and After, I saw that there had passed a second "After," the one that set me safe again. The man's loose shirttails and unshaven face caused no concern. He carried a fly rod in one hand and a creel in other. We raised our hands in greeting and made our way back to our snug and separate camps.

10

SUMMERS AND WINTERS PASSED and while the mountains offered consistency, the office was in a state of upheaval. Along with Edie and Sam, other friends dispersed. Ann, the archeologist who worked for me, resigned her position to study aikido in Japan. Another friend quit his forest planning job and moved to Whitefish to teach skiing. Sara, my first and finest friend since I had arrived in Montana, abandoned her status as combat biologist to stay home and care for her five acres of newly planted shade trees. The biggest blow was the day Ross announced his retirement.

He had grown uncharacteristically irritable during the months leading up to his announcement and often looked weary and defeated. More than once he said to me, "I don't think I can keep doing this." I assumed he was referring to his need to sit at a desk with a case of sciatica that had worsened to the point where I often found him lying on his office floor with a stack of papers and the telephone beside him.

In the years when I worked for the Gallatin National Forest, computers emerged from their climate-controlled closets to become ubiquitous and necessary tools, a terminal on every desk. A program called Forest Level Information Processing (FLIP) was decreed and soon we were learning how to send messages and documents and to replace our overstuffed file cabinets with electronic copies. Ross was accustomed to scribbling draft memos on lined legal paper and tossing them into his outgoing mail. One of the clerks would stop by in a day or two to have him review the typed memo and sign it. Now he was being asked to compose his letters on the computer and e-mail them for formatting and preparation for signature. I overheard him arguing with the administrative officer in a voice so whiny it sounded as if he might break into tears.

"You mean I have to type my own letters? I went to forestry school—I'm not a secretary."

The AO muttered something in a soothing tone, as if trying to settle a balky horse.

"You can't be serious," Ross said.

More soothing talk.

"Forget it. I'm not doing it."

For a while Ross and a number of others kept sending handwritten memos to the typing pool, but soon there was no mail clerk to pick up the scribbled memos and no typing pool to prepare them, and the old-timers had no choice but to adapt. It was the first of many changes that would result in field time being replaced by hunting and pecking over keyboards and filling out indecipherable forms. This was decidedly not Gifford Pinchot's Forest Service.

In his career Ross had ridden with outfitters into wilderness camps, skied with Jean-Claude Killy when Big Sky Resort first opened, and tromped around in a hardhat with timber purchasers. Increasingly his job consisted of press conferences, rancorous public meetings, and lately, training sessions designed to turn dirt foresters into sensitive 1980s guys. "I can't handle that touchy-feely crap," he declared.

The Forest Service was changing, reluctantly and painfully, as citizens demanded different things from the land and its managers. Controversy dogged the steps of the public affairs officer, point man for complaints of all kinds. Ross found himself having to defend decisions he disagreed with and the Forest Service was no longer a comfortable refuge for men with similar backgrounds, education, and values.

Ross came to my defense on numerous occasions, railing at the engineers for their straight-line roads, at the foresters for their square clearcuts. "You've got a landscape architect on the staff, why don't you use her?" he demanded. Although thoroughly steeped in the traditional culture of the agency, he possessed a unique ability to reach out and understand others. His eyes flashed when I told him people had been saying I was hired only for my gender. "I hired you because you had the best application," he replied. When I finally got around to telling him that the women who worked for him were referred to as "Ross's crack crew" he was able to sooth my ruffled feathers while chuckling at the joke. He stood as a bridge between cultures, someone who wanted people to get along. But the cultures were becoming increasingly polarized, the gap between them ever greater. Worse, the touchy-feely crap continued and eventually Ross wore down. What shoved him over the edge was the new forest supervisor, a computer geek from the Washington office who had been instrumental in the development of FLIP.

The retirement party was packed with Forest Service people from all over the state, social friends and well-wishers from the local community. Environmentalists, timber company executives, newspaper reporters, and outfitters came to say goodbye to Ross. What would the future bring, in a changing work environment where people asked unseemly questions and flaunted their disregard and irreverence toward time-honored Forest Service traditions, where the edict to embrace diversity had resulted in a good deal of resentment and backlash? My life raft was leaving, and I was left to tread uncertain waters.

As it turned out, Ross might have stuck it out. The computer geek didn't last long as supervisor and soon it was announced that his replacement would be the man who had kept us all entertained with his hilarious quips as master of ceremonies at Ross's retirement party, a flush-faced Scots-Irish jokester from Butte who was currently supervisor on an adjacent forest.

The hydrologist who had asked if I was a bra-burner looked shaken when he got the news. "Not my kind of management style," he said. "I'm out of here." Steve was on his way to the Southeastern Region in Atlanta by the time Bob Gibson arrived. I would have done well to follow Ross's sage advice to lie low in the brush, having absorbed the information I needed about Gibson from a photograph hanging on his office wall. The ranger-staff team of his former forest posed for a group shot, taken outdoors in a grass field as if they were a football team. The taller men stood at attention in crisp uniforms while the front row hunkered on one knee with their hands clasped over the other, ready to run for a touchdown.

After Ross's departure, Gibson determined it was unreasonable to ask one person to cover both public affairs and a large, complex recreation program. Because the regional office in Missoula (as well as his former forest) was organized with recreation and lands in the same staff group, he decided the forest should follow suit, thus allowing the lands staff to take on extra duties and extra pay while eliminating the need to advertise and fill two new positions.

The management style of the lands staff who now became my boss was also represented by his office décor. No uniformed football teams for him: over his desk hung a white man's wet-dream image of an Indian woman, her face belonging to a brown-skinned baby doll, her low-cut buckskin dress revealing substantial breasts. I wasn't sure how I would be able to sit across from this picture and brief Mike on something of importance in the recreation program.

On the other hand, we had gotten on well enough. He struck me as an arrogant wiseass—the kind of person I normally enjoyed—and from what I could tell, he loved his job and the forest. Mike had been the lands officer in the early 1980s when the Church Universal and Triumphant bought the Forbes Ranch, a prime parcel of grizzly bear habitat and big game winter range on the margin of Yellowstone National Park. He was brought to tears at the office when the church bought the land out from under the Forest Service, in the midst of a purchase agreement with the Nature Conservancy. After the church took over the ranch, it became a blight on the landscape, with dorms and bunkers and high fences to keep the elk and bison out of what recently had been their home.

As well, Mike could be wildly funny. I sat in his office one day waiting for him to get off the phone, and noticed over my shoulder an older fellow in a polyester twill suit and a cowboy hat full of feathers that made him look like a real estate agent. He stood impatiently outside Mike's office door, also waiting for an audience. When Mike hung up the telephone he glanced apologetically my way then took a look at the character outside the doorway and asked, "Who's this bimbo?" A moment later Mike's assistant introduced him to US representative Ron Marlenee.

Things changed between us when he became my boss. I bristled over being told what to do by someone who knew the recreation program far less well than I did. He belittled my work, calling my scenic resource monitoring "running around the forest taking pictures." Sitting in the office doing his bidding was more important. The forest-wide wilderness education program ended, and with it so did my enthusiasm.

Along with the changes in local management, the national forests and parks had begun to feel the effects of Reagan administration policies. James Watt's notorious effort to sell large parcels of land in the public domain included the entire Crazy Mountains. There was a less trumpeted but more influential shift in funding emphasis that placed commodity production at the top of the list of multiple uses. The forest was being asked to flaunt forest plans, laws, and regulations. But Gibson valued only loyalty, by which he meant loyalty to the outfit, not to the resource or the citizens, many of whom he considered the enemy.

Rainbow Lakes on the Lake Plateau, Absaroka-Beartooth Wilderness.

As the undercurrent of mistrust and paranoia at the forest increased, so did the overt antagonism toward employees who were considered disloyal. I was brash and outspoken and didn't mince words when I had an opinion, and I reacted to the increasingly hostile work environment by becoming more disagreeable. The strain was unraveling me both at work and at home.

As much as I loved Montana, and my home and friends there, I began to search for a new start in another place. Most of the vacant positions posted on the Forest Service website lacked interest for me, isolated towns like the one in Oregon I had escaped, or big cities surrounded by freeways. At last I found a new position advertised, for a resource assistant on the same ranger district where I had taken my first seasonal job as an undergraduate: Sedro-Woolley, Washington. I applied, and as the weeks passed my anticipation grew. I dreamt about the things I had loved to do when I lived in that country, the place where Don and I had first met. Paddling the Skagit River, backpacking in the North Cascades, and wandering the tidal mudflats on rainy winter mornings with snow geese, trumpeter swans, bald eagles, and snowy owls.

Months passed without a phone call from Washington, and eventually I learned the position had been filled. I called the personnel office to ask where I had fallen short and how I could improve my application to compete better next time. The person I talked to was unusually frank. I had been the top candidate until my superiors at the Gallatin National Forest told the district ranger in Washington that I was not a "team player."

Despairing of being able to land another Forest Service job with my obvious lack of support, I sought positions with Montana State University, the US Postal Service, whatever I could find that would allow me to stay in Bozeman. And I spent my time visiting favorite haunts in the backcountry, preparing myself to say good-bye.

At the Hyalite Creek trailhead, I parked the Forest Service truck under a tall Engelmann spruce. A discarded walking stick was propped against the trail sign, the only evidence that anyone had been there recently. Glad to have the mountains to myself on that cloudy weekday morning, I folded a supply of campsite inventory forms into a Ziploc bag, strapped my fire shovel with its cut-off handle onto the back of my rucksack, and hefted the load onto my back. I tugged the waist strap tight to minimize bouncing and started up the trail.

Emotional turmoil had become habit. The wary standoff with my boss Mike had erupted into a shouting match in the office the week before, and in desperation I had paid my first visit to a counselor.

The counselor smiled indulgently. Her dimpled cheeks and nest of blond curly hair reminded me of Shirley Temple. She was kind but unhelpful, telling me I seemed well-balanced and didn't need a counselor. Part of me sighed with relief; the wiser part raised an eyebrow. I called another number. The second counselor was not so sweet and naïve. Her eyes penetrated from a stern face as I talked about what I saw as my problems. She asked, after I had spent ten minutes in her office, "Do your parents drink?"

I stared at her, not comprehending, since I had been talking about my job. "Well, yes," I finally stammered. "They're both alcoholics. What does that have to do with me?"

Amazingly, she didn't laugh. She heard what the first counselor had not, and read the subtext in what I had been telling her. I wanted to know more.

"You're playing out the relationships you had with your parents as a child," she said. "The same patterns will repeat themselves until you understand what lies at the bottom. Coming to a counselor was a good first step."

"What's the second," I asked.

"Keep coming." She also suggested I attend meetings of a group I had never heard of, called Adult Children of Alcoholics.

"Is it that big a deal?" I asked. "I feel selfish just coming to see you."

"You need to start being more selfish."

My mother's words came back to me like a fist in the sternum: *You selfish little bitch.* An accusation guaranteed to leave me devastated. She had known which buttons to push when she wanted my attention, but she had never told me how to be other than what I was, a confused and struggling child. What had I done that had been so unacceptably selfish? What was I supposed to do instead? I never found the answer.

What the counselor meant by selfish was something completely different. I needed look inside, with neither narcissism nor self-loathing, but with open, honest scrutiny. The thought of becoming more self-aware did not appeal at the time, for I was thoroughly tired of myself. But I was willing to try. I had played a part in my own troubles, and I needed to sort out which parts were mine to correct.

The counselor did not smile or try to make me feel better, and I left her office angry. Not at her but at myself, for failing to grasp how deep the hole I had dug for myself had become, and how much effort it would take to climb out. The first thing I needed was to find a forest trail where I could be alone.

I had been running five miles a day since the snow left the Gallatin Valley in April. After a few minutes of warming up I would find the unconscious stride that let my mind shift into neutral, empty of disturbing thoughts. I ran for escape, for the comforting chemicals released by my brain and the sense of clarity they gave. And thus on the Hyalite Trail, I broke into a jog.

Soft and familiar as an old sweater, the trail embraced me with its dusky forest as the patch of daylight at the trailhead receded to a distant point. The creek was a muted prattle beneath a thicket of alder as my footfalls thudded on packed earth. Otherwise the forest was silent. I trotted along in search of the miraculous stride whose rhythm would offer escape from the tempest in my brain.

A loud burst of machine-gun chatter startled me. A squirrel clung to a spruce trunk and scolded vigorously, peering at me with its tail curled into a question mark. It seemed to ask, "Jumpy today, are we?" Then the squirrel scuttled up the tree.

Yes, jumpy. And irritable. I needed a few miles of running to calm myself as the recent fight with my boss kept playing in my mind. I had gathered some special-use regulations for him to read before meeting with the outfitter association and later noticed that I had forgotten an important piece of information. Hurriedly I copied it with a note to alert him, but I must have been too late, for he had gone to the meeting without the needed information and came back to the office steaming mad.

"What kind of crappy staff work is that?" he demanded.

"I left you a note—"

"Liar," he shouted, in front of everyone in the office.

I tried again to explain.

"You lie!" He turned on his heel and stomped out.

I hooked my thumbs into the shoulder straps of my rucksack and increased my pace as if to outrun the dreadful scene in my mind. Once or twice I glanced at the firm muscles pumping below my hiking shorts. Normally I noticed them with pride, glad for the ease with which they took me up a mountain trail. But at the moment even my physical fitness failed to bring a measure of satisfaction. However strong, those legs would never take me away from my failures.

After three miles the gentle trail abandoned the creek's dawdling meanders and alder thickets and began the more serious work of climbing a mountain. Forced to watch my step on the narrow, rocky track, I felt the labor of my breathing and the moisture collecting under my rucksack. The early morning clouds withdrew and bright rays spilled over the canyon rim from the high cirque above. The forest of spruce gave way to isolated stands of subalpine fir with open slopes that marked the paths of winter avalanches. Clusters of sunlit Indian paintbrush flared like torches on the mountainside above, showing me the way, leading me around each switchback as I climbed upward through the thinning mist and into the light.

I had learned to combat side stitches by carefully inhaling over a three-step sequence and exhaling over the next three. Now with a shortened stride against the steep trail, I reined in my breathing to match my feet, counting the rhythmic steps as I took each measured breath. The focus needed to achieve this cadence pushed other thoughts away as my tight canter sent me up another switchback, and another. Soon I had attained the level of the backlit paintbrush flowers. The lower trail and trailhead were far behind me now, lost somewhere in the mist-clad forest.

At last the slope broke and I crossed onto the rim of the wide cirque that held Hyalite Lake. I paused for a moment to count five waterfalls, one so close it filled the air with its noise while the others tumbled from distant rims, gushing white but silent. The brink where I stood was sheltered only by the sky. The sky, my destination.

Along the floor of the cirque basin the paintbrush spread a palette of scarlet, magenta, tangerine orange, and pale yellow. One kind grew short and dense, another tall and spiky. I catalogued their details and tried to separate the species. With the strenuous climb behind me, variations on a paintbrush theme became the sole focus of my interest. I couldn't recall exactly when my mind had left behind Mike and his false accusations, or the counselor with her penetrating eyes and unwelcome questions, but I noticed now that they had faded into the far corners of my mind and in their place was sweet relief.

The sun floated high over the volcanic peaks of the northern Gallatin Range and I guessed it must be close to noon. At Hyalite Lake I dropped my rucksack, splashed into the water, and poured cool handfuls over my

Hyalite Peak and Lake, Gallatin Range, 1986.

head, then found a log seat and pulled the water bottle from my pack. The water was still cold, unopened. I took a long drink and assembled lunch.

Hyalite Lake was a shallow saucer of turquoise set into the bronze of a late-August meadow. A lone spotted sandpiper flew along the water's edge like a skipping stone. Above the lake, an amphitheater of rimrock cupped the sky. Ribbons of alpine rush reached into the talus on the crest of the Gallatin Range, where even at midday the peaks cast long shadows. The sun's warmth soaked into my legs and a cool breeze crept along my spine. The coil inside me continued to unwind, leaving only a vague weariness and no words of condemnation rattling in my head.

Food and rest refreshed me. The lake was lovely, an adequate destination, but after spending an hour cataloguing conditions at lakeshore campsites and finding only enough trash to fill a Ziploc bag, I craved higher ground. The main trail zigzagged up the shoulder of Hyalite Peak. I considered it before remembering a little-used route leading to Hyalite Ridge and the divide with Squaw Creek.

The unmarked path skirted knobs of bedrock and dipped into lush basins filled with delicate hairgrass, monkeyflower, and paintbrush. As the hairgrass meadow grew into thick turf the trail disappeared. No blazes scarred the trees, no rock cairns pointed the way. I scanned the mountain to the west for clues, then plunged toward the base of a boulder slope. The same attention that had shown me variations in paintbrush served me now at the far end of the meadow, for I found the trail slanting up a hem of scree.

Again I climbed, but slower now, tired and exhilarated from my five-mile run. Slabs of cleaved-off bedrock formed the trail, ringing like platters of china underfoot. The talus was loose, still shuffling down the mountain and collecting no soil. Some of the boulders contained holes formed by gas bubbles trapped when the molten basalt cooled and thickened. The vesicles had since filled with a pearly white form of opal called hyalite, namesake of this mountain refuge. The hyalite blinked from the dull gray slabs and pearls of it littered the trail. I picked one up and held it into the light, where it flickered with a trace of pale carmine fire.

As I approached the top of Hyalite Ridge, a long sinuous spine running between Mt. Bole and Hyalite Peak, the slope became gentler, the boulders no longer on the move. Angular slabs settled into nests of rush and mountain heather and clumps of purple-flowered sky pilot. The skunky aroma of its foliage underfoot followed me as I turned the final switchback where the trail squeezed through a cliff band and onto the divide.

A sky full of mountains bounced into view. To the west, the Spanish Peaks bristled with spires. Squaw Creek ran from the west slope of Hyalite Ridge, its upper reaches hidden by the curvature of the mountain on which I stood. In the shelter of its cirque basin far below, Hyalite Lake lounged, a pool of Caribbean green, while shadows crept like timid swimmers from the shaggy pines along its shore. Scanning the distant ranges, I counted over a dozen peaks where I had stood earlier that summer.

The trail began its long drop into Squaw Creek and I abandoned it to stay on the ridge, strolling along with a light and casual step. I had reached my destination, at ten thousand feet in the Montana sky. A block of basalt presented itself before me, the perfect seat. I dropped my pack and drank again, then sat with my hands on my knees, staring. How long had it been since I ran up a mountain and no one knew where I was? I could lie back in the heather and stare at nothing for the next hour, or walk for miles down the crest to the summit of Hyalite Peak, catch the trail, and make a loop back to the trail junction at Hyalite Lake. Either way, for these few hours I had disappeared. With no one probing or peering over my shoulder—*Liar! Do your parents drink?*—I began to enjoy my own company. I wanted nothing, my mind uncluttered and clear.

My once-troublesome side stitches nearly vanished after I learned how to breathe in rhythm with my stride. Now I saw a way to use that idea to combat brain-stitches: get the mind in rhythm with the body. As my legs focused on their task of taking me up a mountain the rest of me had to cooperate. This was no place for the brain to be off on some melancholy tangent; its job was to watch for rocks in the trail and the varying details of Indian paintbrush.

A realization began to seep in: I wasn't running away from my problems anymore, but toward a solution. Moments of clarity, when lungs and heart and legs and mind worked together, were accumulating in my memory, and each day in the mountains added to the inventory.

I understood that the Gallatin National Forest was indeed a boys' club into which I would never gain entry. But neither would women like Nancy, who might be promoted but would mostly be used, manipulated, and put on display to make top management feel self-satisfied. Like other strong, intelligent women I had worked with, she would go along instead of bucking the system in hopes of remaining in favor. But there was always a risk that, in spite of ingratiating her organizational superiors, she would be abandoned. I was, by nature, too stubborn and willful to accept such a bargain.

Beyond this circumstance, I began to see the role that women like Nancy played in my life, as did certain men whom I had found attractive. They were stand-ins for my father: charming on the surface, affable to strangers. But remote, guarded, and ultimately unknowable. As my parents grew distant from each other, Dad withdrew from the family. Most of my high school friends were unaware that I had a father, he showed his face so rarely. Now, in my early thirties, I saw people like Nancy as surrogates in my efforts to win him over. It was not my father himself, but my deep emotional reaction to his persona, that I had begun to plumb.

On the other hand, people like my current boss, who found nothing good in me or my work, and with whom I argued defiantly and openly, represented my mother. Her reprimands were delivered in the form of name-calling and general condemnations, not as guidance toward acceptable behavior. She was frequently angry, and anger became the language with which we communicated.

Once I understood that my defiance toward Mike was a charade of the push-pull relationship I had with my mother, I disliked him less. It wasn't his fault that he had become another person in my life through whom I was trying to work out long-buried emotions. The core of the relationship, not the person involved, was what mattered in my interior exploration. At some murky psychological level, we were all milling around in a costume room, trying out for parts in one another's lives. The counselor was onto something important, I realized, and my moment of insight on a mountaintop came as a major revelation. I felt like a newly winged adult insect, emerging from its brittle carapace.

The image of shedding skin gave me an idea. I untied my boots and pulled them off. Cool air bathed my feet as I peeled off my sweat-damp socks and laid them on a rock, wriggling my toes into the soft mats of heather. It felt delicious and I wanted more. I laid my Forest Service shirt aside, pulled the tank top over my head, and slipped out of my hiking shorts and underwear.

I left my clothing and boots piled neatly on a rock and walked away, bare as the day I was born. What was I doing? Had I lost my mind at last? It didn't feel crazy, and it might have been the sanest thing I had done all summer. With my mind utterly still and my sense of propriety on furlough, my senses were allowed a rare feast. I executed an abbreviated sun salutation and at the end I raised my arms to feel the blessing of warmth on skin stretched tight across my collarbone. A breeze lifted the fine hairs

II

1988. THE YEAR I MOVED FROM MONTANA TO WYOMING was a time of change, filled with intensity—both for myself and the Yellowstone region. When I search through journals from that time I find notes about the travails of packing and moving and house-building, farewells to friends, and what it was like to commute between Jackson Hole and Bozeman via Yellowstone when a third of it was burning.

On the first of May I received an unexpected call from the Bridger-Teton National Forest in Wyoming. A man introduced himself as Al and asked if I might be available for a detail.

"From what we've heard you have the skills we're looking for," he said.

"How'd you get my name?" I pictured him sitting at his desk, flipping through a Forest Service directory.

"Louisa Willcox," he answered matter-of-factly. "She mentioned that you might be looking for something new."

I held the phone away from my ear and stared at it. Louisa was one of the cursed environmentalists with whom I had been observed having lunch. This fellow Al had called because of a recommendation from the enemy?

"How do you know her?" I asked.

"She's highly respected in the Jackson area. I'd call her a friend."

Before moving to Bozeman for a position with the Greater Yellowstone Coalition, Louisa had worked for the Jackson Hole Alliance for Responsible Planning, a nonprofit that paid close attention to the development of the Bridger-Teton National Forest's plan. Louisa had told me about her work and cordial relationship she enjoyed with the forest staff, but I was still stunned: not only was she well regarded by the Forest Service, she had called to put in a good word for me. The Jackson Hole office had to be a different agency than the one where I worked.

"It sounds great," I said. "You want me when?"

"Monday, if possible. Who should I call to arrange it?"

Amazingly enough, Mike balked.

"Not sure if we can afford to let you go," he told me.

"Aren't you dying to get rid of me?" I asked. "If it weren't for you, I'd be in Washington by now."

A few phone calls and one week later, I traveled to Jackson Hole to begin my detail with the forest planning team. I went with a blend of eagerness and apprehension, my wary antennae extended to test the work environment and management style, for I knew there was a vacant position on the staff and if I pleased my new employers it might be offered to me.

Louisa had told me she was impressed by the attitudes she encountered among the Bridger-Teton staff, newly reorganized to form what was called the ecology resources group. Al, a former wildlife manager and game warden, was the staff officer in charge. "They have a wildlife biologist running the timber shop," Louisa said incredulously. From my perspective the Bridger-Teton offered the gift of a new start, another chance, and the possibility that I still possessed skills that somebody wanted.

Yet. Perhaps it was the music of the word Montana, a state whose name meant mountains, the place in which I had discovered Greater Yellowstone. As I contemplated uprooting myself from the sweet wild country north of Yellowstone I lost much sleep, unable to tell what worried me more—that I would be offered a permanent job in Jackson Hole, or not.

As I contemplated the alternatives, I thought the choice should have been easier. I was discontented with my current situation, but people embrace the familiar, and much of what was familiar was also dear to me. I told myself I needed to go elsewhere and start over if I meant to gain the clarity I had glimpsed during my run to Hyalite Ridge, a clarity that left me hungry for more. Running away was no escape, for I'd be taking my same old self along, while a physical move would perforce give me a new perspective. And thus the internal argument continued as I began my four-month detail.

While Don stayed home and took care of the garden, the weekly commute between Bozeman and Jackson became routine. On the way south I drove past steaming geysers and greening meadows and newborn bison calves bucking and running circles around their placid mothers. Near Yellowstone National Park's South Entrance came the first view of the Teton Range, a picket fence of spires still clad in winter's snow. But as I closed in on Jackson, I began to feel a familiar tightness in my chest. I knew little about my new workplace other than the standard wisdom—Jackson was a tourist trap where drunken rednecks at the Cowboy Bar hauled longhairs into the town square to whack off their ponytails.

The Tetons kept tugging at my eye and I stopped beside Jackson Lake to surrender to the stunning view. I had seen those mountains for the first time in the spring of 1974, when a field course in geology took me across the arid West. Toward the end of our spring quarter tour, we drove north to Grand Teton National Park, where the scent of sun on lodgepole pines and a fresh breeze blowing off the mountains felt like homecoming after living for weeks in desert landscapes. Now I rolled the window down to catch that piney scent again. It drifted into the car along with this reassurance: I remained in the country known as Greater Yellowstone, my adopted home range. Starting anew after a history of personal failures, I realized I had been given an uncommon gift, the chance to sweep clean the past and learn from my mistakes. In Jackson Hole, I was free to be a learner, the new employee with no baggage. Humbled by past experiences, I was eager to do better.

The essential task of my detail was to write a cogent justification for declaring some of the Bridger-Teton National Forest off limits to energy exploration. The forest plan was nearing completion and it had already been decided which of the 1.5 million acres of inventoried roadless area were to be managed for primitive recreation and wildlife habitat. Yet there was the prickly issue of oil and gas, which operated under its own rules, and like all mineral resources it was where you found it, however scenic or wild the land.

"We can't tell the public we're going to keep these areas wild with no roads or timber sales, then open it to oil and gas," the forest supervisor said. "But industry deserves a clear explanation if we're going to slap a no-lease regulation on them."

I hunkered at a computer in an empty conference room, gathered my reference materials, and started to write what I hoped would be a clear explanation. It was lonely work, and I was glad for meetings of the forest planning team, a convivial crew who seemed to find something to laugh about no matter the topic at hand. We gathered at an unused bunkhouse we called the planning shack, at the far edge of the forest headquarters compound, and went about the work of completing the 400-page Bridger-Teton National Forest Land and Resource Management Plan and the accompanying environmental impact statement, twice the size of the plan. On a deadline imposed by the regional office, we frequently worked

Teton Range from the Snake River, 1988.

into early evening. After work I walked until sundown and went home to my kitchenette motel room a half-block from the supervisor's office. On Friday afternoons, I tried to leave Jackson early enough to arrive in Bozeman before dark.

On one trip north near the end of June, I found traffic stopped on the highway near West Yellowstone while a helicopter trailing a canvas bucket swooped low over our heads, carrying water scooped from Grayling Creek. Smoke rose beyond the forested slopes on the east side of the highway, the first of many plumes that would fill the sky that summer. With the distance of decades, the wildfires of 1988 now seem ecologically benign rather than a destructive force devouring the world's first national park. That was hardly the case at the time.

Yellowstone and the forests surrounding it are dominated by lodgepole pine, spruce, and subalpine fir, much of it well over two hundred years old. Fire is a natural part of the ecosystem and typically the fire season begins in late summer, around the first week in August. The years of 1986 and 1987 had seen record drought in some parts of the region, and 1988 started out dry as well. The lime-green understory foliage north of Grayling Creek was deceptively reassuring. The smoke that rose beyond those frontal hills would soon be named the Fan Fire, one that burned for the rest of the summer and grew to more than 27,000 acres.

As it happened, the Fan Fire was the smallest of the many named fires, most of which eventually burned into one another to become complexes. The fires were mostly ignited by lightning, although the Huck Fire that started near Yellowstone's south entrance started when a wind gust blew down a power line. The Huck Fire began on August 20, 1988, thereafter referred to as Black Saturday. While members of our planning team made jokes about whether to call the Huck Fire a natural fire (wind) or human-caused (the power line), the rest of Yellowstone went up like a torch. The acreage involved in fires currently burning in the park increased by more than 50 percent. Flame length, a measure of fire severity, exceeded two hundred feet under the force of the wind. Thunderheads of smoke billowed thirty thousand feet into the air.

Sequestered in the planning shack, our team declared unavailable for fire assignments, we spent the summer watching from afar. I monitored the ruddy cloud of smoke that defined the northern horizon. Each day the cloud grew larger as the Mink Creek fire overtook the Emerald Lake burn, then both joined the Huck Fire and coalesced into a massive burn called the Snake River Complex. It looked as if the entire Teton Wilderness was engulfed in fire.

Firefighters' reports crackled over the Forest Service dispatch radio. The situation was out of control—a gust of seventy knots had advanced a fire front ten miles in an hour. On the television news, flaming trees exploded beside Old Faithful Inn while crews soaked the wood-shake roof with fire hoses in a desperate effort to save it. As travel through the park became too dangerous the roads were closed and I commuted to Bozeman via the highway to the west, from which I could overlook the Madison Plateau, filled with glimmering points of red light from fires that sent smoke into the sky on the scale of a volcano.

The inferno was quenched the second week of September. After months of smoke and helicopters and slurry bombers, of grimy toil by thousands of firefighters, it came down to the secret weapon that snuffs most wildfires in the Rocky Mountain West: snow.

When Yellowstone reopened I slipped away to have a look. I braced myself for a shock while hoping it wouldn't be as bad as I imagined. As I topped the hill north of Jackson the Tetons burst into view, the air between us clear for the first time since the middle of July. The menacing thunderhead on the northern skyline was gone.

The first burns crossed the road at Nickel and Dime Creeks in the J. D. Rockefeller Parkway. I drove past blackened trees that ran from roadside to rimrock. Once inside Yellowstone Park I gaped at the change since the last time I'd driven through: all that remained of the lush willows along the Snake River were clusters of charcoal-black wands. The Lewis River Canyon was a fire-scoured chimney. Beyond its cliff-lined inner gorge, branchless spires smudged the mountainsides for as far as I could see in both directions. The Lewis River, clear and blue, tumbled through the devastation, looking strangely out of place.

I slowed at one of the river overlooks, thinking I had seen quite enough. It wasn't too late to cancel this depressing expedition and turn back. But I pressed on, out of some kind of morbid curiosity, and abruptly found myself driving through a robust, snow-flecked forest. The road rolled over gentle ridges where young lodgepole pines crowded its shoulders, their branches turned upward as if in thanks and jubilation.

At the north shore of Yellowstone Lake I stopped to look in the direction I had come. The fire that had scorched the Lewis River canyon spread deep into the rumpled hills beyond, up the flanks of Mt. Sheridan, across the basin that held Heart Lake, and over Mt. Hancock, Big Game Ridge, Two Ocean Plateau: a landscape of charcoal and powdered ash, an ecological clean slate. Ahead of me the burn diminished to fingers stretching into large blocks of untouched forest. Black patches with bronze haloes spattered a canvas of green, the classic "mosaic" pattern of a natural wildfire as it burned selectively, taking stands of old, insect-ridden pines and skipping over moist areas and places where the trees were young and full of the juice of life, not yet ready to burn. Elsewhere, the fire had crept along the forest floor, leaving the trunks blackened but unharmed, the tinder of dropped branches cleared away.

Yellowstone's Central Plateau—high, moist, and mantled in a forest of mixed conifers—had not burned at all. At Old Faithful and farther down the Madison, the forest had burned as intensely as it has in the Lewis River canyon. To my eyes the transition from mature woods to barren ground was stark and shocking, but this ecosystem worked on a scale and timeline I could scarcely comprehend. Its evidence lay in the unburned stands that climbed to the farthest ridges. They appeared at first glance to be a continuous carpet of lodgepole pine but a closer look

New pines growing in the Lewis River Canyon, Yellowstone National Park, six years after the 1988 fires.

revealed a subtle mosaic, an interwoven texture of various-aged stands, the younger ones recognizable by their ferny texture and light yellow-green while swaths of old growth stood dark and shaggy within them. The newly burnt patchwork of black snags with their amber haloes followed the same pattern. Like it or not, this was how the world worked in Yellowstone. However brutal the immediate aftermath, fire was less an agent of devastation than of renewal.

Like most people, I thought of natural change as something that was supposed to happen at the plodding pace of geologic time. In fact, cataclysm had always been an influence, the planet's history a series of thumping by meteors and submersion in the smoke of volcanoes. Such events were not confined to the distant past, though their infrequency lulled us into believing so. A creature with a life span of less than a century can form dynasties and civilizations in the interstices of geologic time.

In Yellowstone the dominant forest tree, lodgepole pine, uses fire to its advantage. The trees start as seeds in serotinous (late-season) pinecones sealed by pitch that only the heat of a forest fire can open. The blackened snags surrounding the roadway were able to sprout and live for two hundred years because of fire. The snags of 1988, twenty-five years later, are now shedding their bark and turning silver with age. People photograph them and call them picturesque while the saplings from their serotinous cones grow up around them.

I made a final stop just short of the Montana line. A bull bison munched cattails beside the roadway, unconcerned with the change in scenery around him; a six-point elk nibbled with apparent satisfaction on a strip of charred pine bark. It occurred to me that I might learn something from their casual acceptance. I turned toward home and for the second time that day I drove through the fires of 1988. The recent burns were huge but they were nevertheless surrounded by miles of reassuring green. Even the Lewis River Canyon looked less ravaged when seen in the context of the whole of Yellowstone. The park was not the same, but it had survived.

As the fires cooled I faced my personal decision. The job offer had come and I had a week to accept or decline. My mind divided into two columns, pro and con, and as the time grew short I focused on the con. I would have to sell the house that Don and I had spent two years building, leave the trees and garden we'd tended, leave the friends and mountains that I loved. After showing some initial enthusiasm for the pending move, Don was getting cold feet over the entire enterprise—the cost of real estate and lumber, the likelihood that we (he) would be building our new house over a long and snowy winter. And though I'd been encouraged by my brief introduction to the Bridger-Teton Forest, I was still head-shy about working for the Forest Service at all. At that point my ideal job ran along the lines of a walking postal route in downtown Bozeman. I'd be outdoors and on my feet all day, and every door I approached would be opened by someone glad to see me.

There were no openings at the post office. What could I look forward to if I declined this offer and returned to the Gallatin National Forest, which had already begun to feel like the distant past? The Montana elk season was about to begin, and forest employees would be recruited to help with hunter patrols—but not me. I was a competent rider but was rarely given a chance. I had learned to stand aside like a rank dude while someone else saddled my horse, and by the time I was considering this move I had come to doubt my ability to handle a task of any size or complexity, whether saddling a horse or forming an intelligent sentence. How could I disappoint the people in Wyoming who were giving me another chance? How could I disappoint myself? Instead of resigning my position in disgust and defeat, as several of my colleagues had done,

I would be moving on to something better, a promotion to a position as a staff officer.

When I was introduced to the Bridger-Teton Forest's leadership team, the group of managers I was about to join as its only female member, I had braced myself for the usual cold stares. Two of the district rangers left their seats to shake my hand. Already they had taken me on pack trips, and I saddled my own horse. What about this career decision did I find so difficult? Like the aging pine forests of Yellowstone, I had to ruthlessly destroy the old to allow the possibility of something new.

I had been vindicated when offered the promotion to the Bridger-Teton. Brian, the forest supervisor in Jackson, told me that when he called the Gallatin for reference checks, Ross had come to my rescue once again.

"I talked to your boss and the forest supervisor," he told me. "What they told me didn't sound right based on what I know about you."

"I'll bet," I said.

"It was odd, they both said the same thing, and I smelled a rat. 'She can't be trusted.' 'She's not loyal—an *environmentalist*.' I told Gibson we wanted someone with ties to the environmental community." Brian laughed, but I couldn't laugh with him as I imagined what else he had probably heard about me.

"So I called Ross," he said. Brian had known Ross for decades and trusted him completely. "Ross told me all that was a bunch of baloney and you were the best employee he'd ever hired."

I nearly cried, wanting to run to Bozeman and give Ross a hug.

What helped me decide on Jackson Hole were two things. First was that stunning range of mountains. The Tetons never failed to draw my imagination, my chin, and my spirits upward. Second, a gentle old lady with silver hair who had lived in the same log cabin at the foot of the Teton Range for nearly fifty years.

When my geology field course camped in Jackson Hole in 1974, a classmate slipped away one afternoon for a visit with a childhood friend of her grandmother's, who had grown up in Alaska. Cathy had invited me to go along and meet this old family friend, but I declined, not wanting to intrude on their private conversation. Much later I realized the opportunity I'd missed. Margaret Murie, along with her husband, Olaus, had written books about the wilderness from Alaska to the Yellowstone Country. *Two in the Far North* recorded their honeymoon, a dogsled trip through the Alaska wilds. *Wapiti Wilderness* captured their months spent in what is

Olaus and Mardy Murie's home in Jackson Hole, Wyoming.

now the Teton Wilderness, studying the Jackson Hole elk herd. Olaus and Mardy helped found The Wilderness Society and their efforts contributed in large part to the designation of the Alaska National Wildlife Refuge. Olaus didn't live to see passage of the Wilderness Act in 1964, but Mardy stood at President Johnson's side as he signed it into law.

The day before I made my decision on whether to move to Jackson, I found myself in Mardy Murie's living room at last. She listened as I rambled on for far too long about my reluctance to leave Montana and my uncertainty that I'd be able to scrape together enough energy and self-confidence to do justice to the job. I must have sounded like a whiny child, but she had spent a lifetime listening to and encouraging young people and she handled me with sympathy and grace. She too had often faced hard decisions, she told me. At the time, I had little understanding of how difficult they had been.

"Sleep on it," she suggested. "I have always found that it's more clear in the morning."

I slept on it and found that she was right. I accepted the job.

12

RACING THE WEATHER AS WE BUILT on one of the last vacant lots in Jackson, Don and I and a few helpful friends installed the roof and windows in time to weather the first serious snowstorms of November. We spent Thanksgiving Day shoveling pea gravel into the basement for concrete delivery the following day, and once in a while we took a break to gaze past the bare cottonwoods to the white slopes of Snow King Mountain three blocks away, where the season's first downhill skiers whooped and hollered. By the end of the following February the house was finished enough to occupy, and it was time for a final trip to Bozeman, where the new woodstove we had purchased was waiting.

The pavement steamed under a strong March sun as Don and I drove west out of Bozeman on Montana Highway 84, the new woodstove in the back of our pickup. A snow squall had passed a few minutes before, leaving the sagebrush beside the roadway bent under a wet heavy mantle of white. The clouds lifted as we reached the Madison River, affording a clear view to our destination: Red Mountain.

The storm must have missed it, or the sun had already melted what snow had fallen, for the mountain looked bare. We turned from the highway at the bridge, bumped along a dirt road for half a mile, and parked.

The air smelled fresh and damp under a warming sun. For the first time all winter I caught the scent of pine and juniper, sagebrush and lichen, joined here by the sweet, fishy smell of algae and decay from the river. The armchair shape of Red Mountain seemed to tilt downward, as if to scoop us into its lap, as we climbed over a sagging barbed wire fence and started up the draw.

We climbed past the lower cliffs and a mid-slope gully where the armchair's upholstery gathered into a narrow pleat, and emerged at the base of a long slope of shattered rock. Platter-sized mats of pink-flowered *Douglasia* covered the talus. I got down on all fours to fill my view with the season's first wildflowers, in bloom before the Equinox, dense masses of deep magenta not an inch above the surface of the ground. Each flower's five petals made a cup that filled with tiny flies.

The tall rock cairn I remembered stood as though it had been waiting for us. Snow cornices clung to the leeward ridgeline, and the surface of the wind-blown snow squealed underfoot, firm enough to hold our weight. We settled beside the cairn and watched the Madison flowing toward us, out of Bear Trap Canyon. I traced the topography with my eye, following Barn Creek into the impenetrable forest where the slope broke into the wide bench lands of Cowboy Heaven. Somewhere in those folds of grass and forest, Dan and Don Nichols had once lived. Perhaps the offspring of their turnips still grew. Somewhere among the grassy folds not so far from where I sat was the site of the pair's last campfire. With the two men now in prison and my move to Wyoming nearly complete, the dark canyon of the Bear Trap lost the sense of foreboding I had found there on my early visits. Now it felt like home again.

As I scanned the mountains surrounding the rock cairn, I understood one painful thing: except as an infrequent visitor, I would not be back. I knew it when I looked across the Madison River to the Spanish Peaks and thought for the last time, *my* wilderness. No, it wasn't mine, any more than it belonged to the street vendor in New York City. But six years of caring for specific places within the vast domain of the national forest had given me a sense of propriety. By places, I meant individual campsites tucked deep into the wilderness.

Among the last field trips I made the previous summer, while still employed by the Gallatin National Forest, was a four-day backpack into the Spanish Peaks, part of the Lee Metcalf Wilderness, with the well-known wilderness researcher David Cole. He was based in Missoula at the Aldo Leopold Wilderness Research Institute, and had written many papers that I relied on for monitoring the effects of human use in wilderness, from weed patches to meadows grazed by pack stock, but mostly focused on established campsites. I wanted to show him those campsites, some of which had all but disappeared, whereas others seemed destined to become permanent and growing expanses of raw earth. The goal was to maintain a few established sites with a minimum of disturbance to soil and vegetation, and ask people to use what the Forest Service called no-trace camping practices. It was a tricky balance to be struck, to minimize the influence of people on the wilderness while allowing them the freedom they sought. Could he suggest anything else to do?

My idea at the time was that if everyone practiced no-trace camping, the wilderness could hold more campers with no damage to the land. Though I'd seen many signs that encouraged me in this belief, I didn't expect that every beat-in campsite in the Spanish Peaks would someday disappear. My friend Judith, who oversaw part of the Alpine Lakes Wilderness an hour's drive from Seattle, told me that everyone in her part of the country was a no-trace camper, but there were still too many of them. The Alpine Lakes was headed for quotas and designated campsites and visitor permits and no-camping zones in an effort to maintain a semblance of wildness at the threshold of a swelling population that stretched from Everett to Olympia. I saw those measures as a necessary admission of defeat. There was no *freedom of the hills* with all these restrictions and the need to plan an itinerary months in advance to assure you had the campsite you wanted on a given night. And, having no city the size of Seattle nearby, I thought we could do better in Montana.

I focused on the inventory, monitoring, and cleanup of wilderness campsites because people spent much of their time in campsites and the conditions found there would influence the experience of visitors. And also because campsites were among the few things the Forest Service could effectively manage. Reducing their size and number, the evidence of soil erosion, the stumps of hacked-off trees and the rusted cans under the skirts of subalpine firs, had concrete results. If nothing else, it would buy time for the Lee Metcalf Wilderness before it had to be managed like the Alpine Lakes.

On our first day in the Spanish Peaks, David Cole and I stopped at a camp in the South Fork of Spanish Creek, beside the trail junction at Pioneer Falls, where I'd taken a "before" photo several years previous. Before, it was a room-sized barren sore spot under a group of lodgepole pines. Now it was part of the meadow, tall with grass and cinquefoil and geranium. We both marveled at the ability of the land to recover from the degree of trampling and soil compaction evident in the photograph, though this was a productive site and relatively few parties wanted to

The author and Wag on the crest of the Spanish Peaks, Lee Metcalf Wilderness, 1984.

camp within so few miles of the trailhead. We continued along Falls Creek to the basin that held Jerome Rock Lakes, where some of the campsites had improved over time while others stayed the same. We found a few new ones in places I had not recorded before.

Ours was a party of three, counting David's Labrador. Few legal campsites could be found in that fragile high-elevation lake basin—legal meaning that they were located at least two hundred feet from water. The lakes themselves were barely two hundred feet apart, so a strict enforcement of the camping setback would effectively close the area to overnight use. Acceptable campsites lay on durable turf and rock slabs well beyond the lakes, but these were large enough only for a party the size of ours. Which prompted a discussion of one of David's main points as he conducted research on the effects of visitor use in wilderness and drew conclusions that he hoped forest managers would use.

Like other wildernesses, the Lee Metcalf had party size limits intended to reduce the damage that camping caused to lakeshores. Most of the campsites had been established decades ago, chosen for their proximity to the lakes and well within the two-hundred-foot setback now in effect. They lay above nine thousand feet and the ground cover was mostly mountain heath and grouse whortleberry, easily broken and killed by trampling. The party size limit in the Spanish Peaks was fifteen people and fifteen horses.

David swept his arm across the lake basin. "Do you see any place that could accommodate a party of fifteen, with fifteen head of stock?"

If a party of that size were camped within sight, it would have resembled a small city. If the group stayed more than a night, an acre of dead whortleberry would be left in their wake.

"To tell the truth, I've never seen that many people in a group," I said. "It's usually three or four."

"Exactly my point. In nearly every wilderness, six is a large group. So why does the Forest Service set limits that are more than twice that number?"

"To accommodate outfitters, I suppose. And the Boy Scouts."

"If you're not willing to set a party size limit small enough to make a difference, why have one at all?"

Good question. I doubted that I would be able to influence the camping party size in the Spanish Peaks during the three weeks that remained of my tenure on the forest. It had seemed a great achievement to get the number down to fifteen.

We moved from one lake basin to another over the next few days, each area presenting its unique challenges for a wilderness manager trying to keep the wilderness wild with as few restrictions as possible. At Jerome Rock Lakes, small parties of no-trace campers could find unused spots for years and cause no damage, but everyone wanted to camp at the same few spots beside the lakes where they had camped for years. It occurred to me that designating campsites, if not for the administrative hassle, would provide what people wanted more than no-trace camping did. And perhaps it would limit damage to fragile vegetation in the high country.

At Lake Solitude, there was only one desirable camp, also too close to the lake. The same was largely true at Spanish Lakes. At the tarn named Beehive Lake, perched at 9,620 feet among the crags, there was no legal campsite at all, unless one was willing to suspend a bivouac sack like a hammock between two blocks of talus. Yet people camped in all these places, and no one complained to the Forest Service about the multiple fire rings or bare patches of earth.

"So, what do you think of going to designated campsites?" I asked. "There are too few choices here and we don't want to close the area to camping altogether."

"Designated campsites are not a bad idea in a place like this," he said. "These sites are never going to look like no one has been here. Look at the results of your monitoring—in the past five years they haven't changed at all."

Other than the trash I packed out, that was true. But it was hard for me to call a long patch of bare earth and chopped-off pines acceptable in wilderness.

"Then your option is to close these camps," David said. "If your managers won't consider that, the next best thing is to tell people to use the established sites, even if they are too close to the water. There's no way they can do more damage—unless of course you have too big a party, like say, fifteen." He grinned.

"Makes sense," I said.

"The campsites that concern me the most are the ones that get used once or twice a season," he said. "It takes very little to push them into a higher-impact category. Those are the ones to watch." He raised his palms at the Spanish Lakes camp. "Come back here in ten years and it will look the same. It'll probably be years before this area will need use quotas, permits, or any of that kind of thing," he said.

Overall, David's comments were encouraging. But the time to reduce the wilderness party size limit or to designate campsites was probably already upon us, before the population of Bozeman doubled. The alternative would be to allow campsites to continue expanding, for the Forest Service to turn its back on its wilderness regulations about where to camp. While the situation presented a conundrum for those in charge of protecting the character of the wilderness, it wasn't as if a patch of bare ground next to an alpine lake was a major threat to the ecosystem. To most people, the bare patch was an advertisement: camp here.

Regardless of what we humans threw at it, Montana would survive, and so would the Spanish Peaks, Ramshorn Lake, the Hilgard Basin, and Hyalite Ridge, all the places I had known and loved, places that offered the gifts of wild, high country—quiet, beauty, and grace. Repose for the world-weary soul. I was satisfied that I had done my best to help, however insignificant the contribution. While gathering trash and

Madison River from the slope of Red Mountain, 1983.

dismantling unneeded fire rings were no more than gestures in the grand scale of the wild earth, they amounted to an acknowledgment of all that I owed the places that had nurtured me.

At the Red Mountain cairn I counted the folds of hazy mountains in the distance, reassured by the span of time implied by those layers of eroded metamorphic rock. By this time I had worked on the staff of the Bridger-Teton National Forest for nearly a year, and the painful memories from my time with the Gallatin had begun to lose their punch. Anger and regrets found their place among those distant layers of rock, represented in the thinnest film of dust. In the familiar and beloved forms of the Gallatin Valley landscape I recognized the cusp where anger melted into forgiveness, like an old cornice of crusty snow on a warm spring day. I recalled the gratifying trips to the mountains, like the one with David Cole, not the arguments in the office.

I stood on Red Mountain with a sense of saying farewell, yet Montana had forever left its mark on me. Don and I descended slowly, taking in the lichen-green boulders and dabs of *Douglasia*, pausing to watch newly arriving bluebirds as they perched on twigs above the straw-blond

13

FROM MAY UNTIL OCTOBER, 1988, forest planning had kept me out of the mountains, and the construction at home demanded all my time in the evenings and on weekends. Eventually the draft forest plan emerged for public review and its authors were released to resume their regular jobs.

In the Intermountain Region, whose regional office is located in Ogden, Utah, the Bridger-Teton Forest was a distant outpost, overlooked in comparison to the Wasatch Front and forests with National Recreation Areas—the Sawtooth and Ashley. And those with large timber programs—the Targhee, Boise, and Payette. The Bridger-Teton was considered too "green" for the taste of many regional staff. The forest plan was grumbled about in the RO for the innovations that won it praise from the public, but it was the only plan in the region for which all appeals were successfully negotiated. It was the only plan to escape challenges in court.

The Bridger-Teton was unique in the region before consolidation joined the Humboldt and Toiyabe National Forests in Nevada; at 3.4 million acres, it was the largest national forest in the lower 48 states, and twice the size of the Gallatin. It differed greatly from the Gallatin in its wide diversity of landscapes and vegetation types, running from Yellowstone Park to Kemmerer, Wyoming, and down the crest of the Wind River Range to its southern foothills.

But the primary difference I saw when scanning a map of the forest was its lack of checkerboard land. Checkerboard ownership patterns, wherein every other square mile was alternately owned, affected well over 100 million acres in the West. In the latter part of the nineteenth century federal grants conveyed entire sections of 640 acres of public land to the railroads, free of charge. Alternating sections of land on

South Cottonwood Creek and Bear Creek, Gallatin National Forest, showing a 640-acre clearcut on private timber land within the national forest.

either side of railroad rights-of-way, extending as far as forty miles from the tracks, were given to the railroads, in part to provide timber for ties, in part because the federal government had hoped to sell the alternating public parcels at higher value.

The legacy of checkerboard land had created enormous problems within the Gallatin National Forest. The federal government was required to grant adequate access to private land within the national forest, so when the Burlington Northern Railroad got into the timber business, the Forest Service allowed it to build roads crossing national forest land to access the private timber. In some watersheds, the private sections were clearcut edge to edge, as can still be seen in the Bear Creek area near the mouth of the Gallatin Canyon. The roads gave access to private land, but the public was not necessarily allowed to drive them, so access to the alternating national forest sections was also restricted by gates. In some places, including Bear Creek, the private land was so completely cleared of timber that the allowable cutover acreage in the watershed was exceeded, thus preventing the national forest from cutting any timber at all until the forests on private lands were declared adequately restocked.

The problems increased when the vision of the original land grant began to reach fruition: instead of the penniless homesteaders envisioned long ago, those who sought to purchase land in the forest were wealthy developers. The railroad-cum-timber companies had no use for cutover lands that would not yield another harvest for many decades, and some of them converted to development interests, or sold the land to those already in the business. Big Sky Resort and its surrounding area serves as an example. A land exchange to consolidate checkerboard land had been in the works since Chet Huntley purchased property near the crest of the Madison Range for a future ski resort.

When Congress authorized an exchange in the Big Sky area as part of the Lee Metcalf Wilderness Act of 1983, the national forest was consolidated in some areas, while the West Fork of the Gallatin River drainage (as well as Jack Creek on the west slope of the mountains, part of the Beaverhead National Forest) was open for private development. What has happened in the area since I left in 1988 can hardly be considered in the public interest. We once hiked to the summit of Lone Mountain, then within the national forest. Now one rides a tram to the top, with a commanding view of some of the densest development in the Northern Rockies. Private ski and golf clubs that advertise based on their exclusivity have replaced public land belonging to all.

In contrast, the Bridger-Teton National Forest contained no checkerboard land within its proclaimed boundaries, and relatively few private inholdings. Most of those inholdings were ranches held by the sons and grandsons of homesteading families. Their presence did not intrude on the surrounding national forest.

While Don and I were building our house, we camped out in Forest Service quarters on the east edge of town. Over the rise above the drafty 1950s-era cabin, where we ate dinner on the living room floor using a cardboard box for a table, lay Cache Creek, whose valley I would come to know well. One day I stumbled onto an informal trail in a tributary called Woods Canyon. At the top of the Cache Creek divide I could traipse across the sparsely forested mountain front to the north and connect with a series of narrow logging roads that hadn't been used in seventy years. From the National Elk Refuge, the same abandoned route climbed in six long switchbacks up the face of the frontal hills a few miles north of town. The loop could be done with a short shuttle involving bikes or a couple of cars and it was one of the first longer excursions I sampled in the Cache Creek area.

Though it lacked a standard destination—no alpine lake or rocky peak—the trail soon became a favorite. On soft summer evenings Don and I hiked the thousand vertical feet through fields of arrowleaf balsamroot and stemless goldenweed, across forested dry gulches thick with Douglas fir, eventually emerging onto an open west-facing slope. Beyond the sixth switchback the trail entered continuous forest. Some of the oldest buildings in Jackson, dating from the early twentieth century, were made from the trees cut on that slope.

From the top of the glade we watched the sun dip behind the Tetons, the broad plain below bright green in June, bronze by August. Most of what could be seen from that vantage point looked as wild as the day before history. Oxbow lakes and lush pastures traced the low spots on the elk refuge where Nowlin Creek met Flat Creek. Sometimes the voices of Canada geese or sandhill cranes rose from the ponds and grassy flats, and we frequently saw elk, coyotes, deer, and bighorn sheep.

Don came to call this viewpoint, where we stood on a four-foot-diameter stump at the edge of the forest, the Burning Bush. The remains of an old-growth Douglas fir, torched by lightning one August afternoon a year after the 1988 Yellowstone fires, the tree was a pillar of flame visible from town. With orders that all wildfires be aggressively extinguished, a hand crew raced up the mountain and cut down the tree while it was still on fire.

In the years since I started watching sunsets from the Burning Bush, more buildings began to dot the valley floor, but the fens and bunchgrass prairies of the refuge still waited below, silent or murmuring under an evening wind, the gentle swells of Miller and Saddle Buttes going sagebrush-gray beyond, the Tetons on the skyline as always, blue in the summer twilight.

In the arid land of Jackson Hole—twenty inches of moisture in a year, and most of that in the form of snow—the mountain folds and faults were scantily clad and the slightest human alterations to the landscape were obvious. Thus the lack of human imprint where the National Elk Refuge met the national forest was startling. Native wild rye, sweetgrass, needlegrass, Indian rice grass, and little bluebunch nodded in the summer breeze. Teton County was, and remains, 97 percent public land, and from the Burning Bush I could see little other than the peaks of the national park, the open grasslands of the national wildlife refuge, and the Douglas fir slopes of the national forest. From such an uncommon perspective the land felt young and vibrant, the mountains freshly chiseled. Flat Creek ran in deep meanders, where twenty-inch cutthroats teased fishermen.

Many people had told me that on their first visit to the Tetons they felt as if they had come home. Even if they never found a way to live here, they inhabited this place, because it lived in their hearts. This kind of inhabitance is as different from simple residence as ancient petroglyphs are from the spatter of a vandal's bullet on a rock. At the Burning Bush I meditated on my good fortune to have lived in a sequence of inspiring wild places, Jackson Hole premier among them. My good fortune to have lived at all felt like nothing short of a miracle.

When I was growing up, I didn't expect to reach the age of thirty. Not only did it seem unimaginably ancient from a child's perspective, I was part of that generation of Americans who drilled for air raids in grade school and shrank away from tabloid headlines at the grocery check-out, each new year heralded by the latest "predictions." The popular psychic Jeanne Dixon warned that the two World Wars had been nothing compared with what awaited us in the distant 1980s.

My father dismissed Dixon as a quack while my mother countered that she had been right before. Psychic or quack, Jeanne Dixon's prediction seemed to me a safe enough bet. I was vaguely aware that our country had nearly started a nuclear war when I was nine years old, over something in Cuba called the missile crisis, at about the same time I witnessed the destruction of the only woodland I had ever known. The 1980s became fixed in my mind as a future to dread.

"I guess I'll start building my bomb shelter in 1979," a neighbor joked from the other side of my parents' card table. "On Vancouver Island, where I'll be upwind."

Of all the overheard adult conversations that took place around the card table, this is the one I remember best. I searched the world atlas for places upwind and decided I would move to New Zealand. In the meantime I crawled under my school desk when the sudden blare of an air-raid siren interrupted class. A room full of first-graders jumped up and pushed our desks into the corner farthest from the windows and dove into the dark refuge underneath. We nudged each other and giggled to distract ourselves from an unimaginable horror as we hunkered down with foreheads, knees, and toes on the floor, hands clasped behind our necks.

The siren-sound that blared from the public-address system did not belong in a room sweetened by the milk-and-graham-cracker scent of children, but there we were, huddled against the polished tile floor while our teacher explained in a calm, airline-stewardess voice that if this were a "real" air raid we could expect a brilliant flash of light followed by the windows bursting. The boys butted each other with blonde crew-cut heads and joked about how cool that would be. I shuddered against the slender warmth of my best friend Diane and waited in silence for the strange, ungodly light that would pierce my clenched eyelids.

A bright female voice soon pronounced the drill over. We scooted our desks back into neat rows and resumed our lessons as if these minutes on the floor were a routine part of the school day. None of us spoke of what had just happened; we believed that speaking of the unspeakable might trigger a nuclear attack with its blinding flash and spraying glass, and the one who broached the subject would be to blame.

Because we couldn't speak of it, the fear went underground. With only a vague notion of the threat that shadowed me at recess, I longed for the dark shelter beneath my desk, an imaginary safety zone where the wars of adults could not reach innocent children. I pretended to enjoy the half-hour of skipping rope or playing four-square with the patched and lumpy rubber ball that Diane had named *Little Awkward* while keeping one distrustful eye on the close, foreboding sky. Even the misty overcast left plenty of room for untold numbers of aircraft, missiles, and bombs to appear without warning. I crept close to the school's warm bricks on the return to the classroom, seeking imagined cover under scant eaves. I scanned the tops of a row of planted maples that marked the borders of allowed outdoor space during recess, the doomed and heedless crows raising a ruckus in their branches. Before the double doors closed behind me I gave the sodden Pacific Northwest sky one last accusatory glance, as if the clouds themselves were to blame for my fear of the sky; as if the outdoors I loved had betrayed me.

For me and many others of my generation, the air raid drills cast a pall over the native hope and optimism of childhood. Part of the trailing third of the baby boom in a region of increasing prosperity, kids my age might have expected a future of nothing but abundance. We might have expected to achieve our dreams as we talked of becoming scientists and astronauts. Reaching for the moon, we found the same science that kindled such ambitions could snuff us in a moment.

On Wednesday afternoons I attended catechism in a cramped room behind the nave where red votive candles flickered at the feet of the Virgin Mary. There I learned that God bestowed upon Moses Ten Commandments in a showy display of His all-powerful nature, descending onto a mountaintop from the heavens as a ball of fire and setting the mountaintop vegetation ablaze. Perhaps it wasn't the untrustworthy sky that caused me to push my school desk into a corner; perhaps it was God Himself, come to punish me and my six-year-old friends, the children of infidels who had not yet learned the rule *Thou shall not kill.*

During my last year of graduate school in Logan, Utah, the calendar turned to 1980. Jeanne Dixon's calamitous decade stood at the door like the Grim Reaper. I was twenty-seven. The Soviet Union had recently invaded Afghanistan. In revolutionary Iran, American hostages marked their seventy-fifth day in captivity. United States and Soviet aircraft carriers steamed toward the Persian Gulf. The Union of Concerned Scientists, an organization devoted to nuclear disarmament, wheeled out its six-foot clock for the television cameras and dramatically moved the giant minute hand ahead. Over the years, with each escalation of the Cold War arms race, the clock had crept ever closer to nuclear midnight. Now it read 11:58.

I felt like a schoolgirl again, waiting under my desk for the blinding flash of light. I stared out the window of my rented house in Utah to pristine Logan Peak, unable to shake the image of snow that would soon fall on that high, wild mountain. Snow, poisonous and radioactive.

Christmas break dragged on. "Peace on earth," read the greeting cards. I spent most of my vacation staring at a thousand-piece jigsaw puzzle, working perhaps a dozen pieces a day as my master's thesis gathered dust in a corner. Immobilized by dread, I concentrated on the puzzle for distraction. When I looked out the window to the January alpenglow on Logan Peak the knot inside me tightened. This beautiful earth. What were we thinking?

Unthinkable: a word the newscasters once used to describe the prospect of nuclear war. But it was hardly unthinkable to my generation; I had been preparing for it since I was six years old.

My paralyzing fear began to fade as classes resumed and routine eased me back into the world. To my astonishment, by the end of the 1980s hope bloomed on all horizons. The Berlin Wall crumbled under jubilant sledgehammers. Democracy seeped like a spring dawn into Eastern Europe and the Cold War was declared *Over*.

One morning in Jackson Hole, I watched a television documentary on the accident at Chernobyl, Ukraine, ten years after reactor number four exploded. Two hundred times as much radiation was released than resulted from the bombing of Nagasaki and Hiroshima. Five thousand Ukrainians—or twenty thousand by some reports—had since died and many more had left their homes to settle elsewhere. Those who remained ate contaminated vegetables and drank radioactive milk. Their babies were born with defects and sickened with thyroid cancer from excessive concentrations of an isotope of iodine. School children did not dive under their desks for practice; they died slowly without fanfare.

Transfixed by the television, I watched for signs of how the forests and wildlife had fared. The newsman made no mention of them. Survivors of Chernobyl stood in the wan northern sunlight for tearful interviews while I scanned the background. Leaves opened with spring just as they unfurled outside my window in Wyoming. Abandoned Ukrainian settlements, left to fade under an irradiated forest, were now being reclaimed by nature. Trees and pasture grass overcame the roadways. Wildflowers bloomed. The countryside around Chernobyl was on its way to becoming wild and young again, a new frontier. It was a hell of a way to preserve vestiges of nature, I thought—to render the land uninhabitable to people. The huge military reservations in the western United States, many of them leftovers from the Cold War, served largely the same function as the contaminated countryside around Chernobyl, as unintentional refuges for the wild.

Over the years the bark has peeled away from the Burning Bush and its surface has turned black with age. More than three decades after 1980, the year I dreaded since childhood, I still climb this forest access trail. The Burning Bush invites me to sit and watch as soft evening colors glide across a land where wild abundance still remains. Like the burning bush

National Elk Refuge and the Tetons from the Burning Bush trail.

of the Old Testament, it is a place where the divine feels close at hand. The Yellowstone region with its national parks and forests and wildlife refuges, constitutes an extraordinary oasis in a polluted, overcrowded world. It is a priceless blessing that anyone can walk or ride a bike for a few minutes from downtown Jackson and enter the wild oasis. It is not a place apart, but a place we are part of. Not unmarked by human hands; the dirt roads and trails, the mossy stumps and flakes of knapped obsidian attest to our long inhabitance of this place. But here we have managed to inhabit rather than to overwhelm. "Man is here," wrote Mardy Murie of her home in Jackson Hole. "But he has not yet laid a heavy hand on his surroundings." May it ever be so.

Though I owe this place my reverent inhabitance, my witness, and my unflagging energy in its defense, like Moses I sometimes hope to go unnoticed, hiding out in the wilderness from the outstretched hand of the world at large, weary of the need for constant engagement. Like Moses who could not hide from God, I feel a voice persisting deep within. *I have a job for you.* A job for all of us: Never find a reason to render land uninhabitable. Never let our children grow up afraid of the sky.

Don nicknamed the stump on the side of the mountain in jest, to commemorate a tree that lightning set ablaze, but the name fits beyond his intention. I use it in much the same way that Moses used the Biblical burning bush—for inspiration, guidance, and the promise of deliverance. On summer evenings, I walk with gratitude up a little-used trail in a young, wild land to the Burning Bush. I receive no tablets or commandments, just a gentle, silent prod. *Look*, a small voice urges. *The world is filled with beauty.*

14

AN EXTRAORDINARY EVENT OCCURRED the winter after Don and I moved to Jackson Hole. I received a letter from my father. He had paid scant attention to me since I was a child, and if he answered the telephone when I called home, he quickly passed the receiver to my mother.

He wrote with news. He had moved out of the house he shared with my mother for nearly forty years. His first letter came in a manila envelope stuffed with newspaper clippings and photographs. With them I found a single page torn from a yellow legal pad, his letter neatly divided into single-sentence paragraphs. The scent of stale cigarette smoke rose from the creases as I pressed the paper flat.

He wrote in clipped sentences, one or two lines per paragraph, imparting information whose underlying meaning I supplied.

- Today I made bean soup. (My translation: *In my own apartment I am allowed in the kitchen! I'm learning to cook.*)
- A stray cat comes every morning for milk. He doesn't come inside. (*I miss Freddy Boy, the orange kitten my child brought home at age ten and begged to keep. Seventeen years later, he died.*)
- Mother is doing fine. (*She and I are both relieved to be out of each other's hair.*)

To the bottom of the page he taped a newspaper horoscope dated the day before he moved into his apartment. *Domestic adjustment featured, could involve actual change of residence.* "Your mother and I get along much better this way," he assured me.

After reading his letter, I settled in with the photographs. The first one pictured a boy I didn't recognize, straddling an air mattress in the last light of a summer evening and riding the wavelets of Puget Sound a few yards from the pebbled ramp of shoreline. The scene was familiar but who was the boy, and why had my father sent me this picture? Nothing was penciled on the back.

The mystery boy clutched the corners of the air mattress and grinned madly at the camera while a knot of adults stood around a barbecue grill in the blurred background, each with a cigarette in one hand and a cocktail in the other. A low-slung brick house hunkered in a nest of clipped junipers, solid as a block of driftwood. Though I hadn't thought of it in decades I instantly remembered that house. The people held dinner parties in late summer when the weather could be counted on to keep the kids outdoors. I would stand at the water's edge and skip stones across the surface while the sun sank like a molten medallion, leaving the air as cool and blue as the water, leaving the scent of salt and seaweed, the murmur of gravel washing back and forth as Puget Sound rolled pea-sized stones like marbles under its toe.

I laid the boy's image aside and reached for the next picture. This one featured me at age two. Dad carried me on his shoulder, his back to the camera. Eyes alert, a thumb stuck in my mouth, I rested my platinum-blonde head in the hollow between his neck and shoulder. Having seen that picture often, it felt as though I remembered the day, a distant moment that transcends all the fights and arguments, the faltering attempts to make amends that followed. The photograph spoke of a style we shared, a quiet space between us where his neck enfolded mine, the two of us facing in opposite directions.

A few years after my mother took that photograph the trajectories of our lives began their long divergence. With my father, lessons rendered in terse paragraphs on index cards replaced our wordless sharing. He instructed me in Morse code, fishing knots, and the correct fingering for his manual typewriter. But after I entered grade school, an unspoken distance settled between us. "I stopped contributing to your education when you were seven," he wrote, as if that explained it all.

By the time I was seven a palpable tension had taken root between my parents. One night I lay in bed awake as their lowered voices drifted along the hallway from the kitchen. My mother's came in broken, wavering tones following by taut silences. I strained to hear—was she crying? I pictured Dad across the table from her, crossing and re-crossing his legs as he lit one cigarette after another, exasperated into wordlessness.

She blurted, "We should never have gotten married."

The author, age two, riding on her father's shoulder, 1955.

I tightened under the sheet. The floor seemed to sag beneath my bed. Her anger stemmed from disappointments I could not understand, but I knew this: although she had achieved much, she expected more from life than her generation of women was allowed. She had earned a bachelor's degree when most Depression-era farm girls didn't finish grade school. During her first years of marriage, with Dad overseas during World War II, she worked as an airline stewardess—a glamorous career in the 1940s that required her degree in nursing. In the end, her early taste of accomplishment lingered as a bitter reminder of all she could have been.

My father flew supplies over "the Hump," an Army Air Corps soubriquet for the formidable Himalayas. Exotic places had been his beat: Burma, India, China. As a child, I begged for permission to touch the brass candlesticks, the intricately carved bracelets of ivory and silver filigree. I stared into the cedar chest where the treasures lay, and pored over an album of photographs, the chronicle of my parents' lives before I was born. Their faces were familiar yet strange, like the boy on his air mattress. One picture showed them standing in front of a DC-3, Dad stiff and regimental in his Army Air Corps uniform and Mother in her American Airlines flight suit, both of them filled with pride and pleasure as they readied to board their separate planes.

Top left: The author's mother, Virginia Lee Marsh, 1944.

Top right: The author's father, Hugh Paul Marsh, 1944.

Right: Virginia and Hugh Paul Marsh, 1944.

The end of the war brought my mother's first enduring disappointment with her marriage, when Dad decided he had had enough of flying and failed to pursue a lucrative career as a commercial pilot. Instead he sold wholesale decorating fabrics in a territory from Alaska to Montana. On Mondays he took off with a load of samples; on Friday afternoons

I stood at the front window, watching for his Rambler to nose into the driveway. My parents grew up in the farming heartland of southern Ohio and Illinois. Dad was a pioneer of sorts, opening a west coast sales territory for an expanding business based in Columbus. He promised Mother that they would soon be heading home, but the night I lay in bed and listened to her weeping we were still in Seattle.

No single event precipitated the falling out between me and my father; he simply withdrew and so did I. We settled into disconnected lives that rarely joined: school and friends for me, business travel and fishing trips for Dad, the spotless house and fading hopes for Mother. More frequent trips to the liquor store for both of them.

The television blared the news at dinnertime, eliminating conversation and giving me something to watch besides my mother's accusatory glances across the table. I learned to eat quickly and excuse myself. Dad excused himself as well, retreating to his favorite bar where he would spend a convivial evening over martinis with his friends. I imagined him in the dim rosy light of the Blockhouse, the life of the party with his appealing smile. I rarely saw that smile at home; he took it where it was appreciated.

As my mother's alcoholism became acute, it briefly brought me closer to my father. One morning after she had gone to the post office Dad and I began to canvass the house for hidden bottles. We had scarcely mentioned the drinking that now began at mid-morning, but we knew exactly where to look. He produced a bottle of Gilbey's gin from the back of her lingerie drawer and I pulled one out of the toilet tank. From a neighbor with small children came a vial of Icapec, guaranteed to induce vomiting. We laced the gin and stowed the bottles as Mother pulled into the drive. The air of conspiracy, a secret held between us like the warm quiet space we once shared, lasted all afternoon. At three o'clock she sighed and said, "I'm not feeling very good, I think I'll lie down." Dad winked; I grinned.

She had nursed the gin so slowly that the Icapec created no dramatic effect. Though our plan had failed, having shared a secret with my father made me feel like a two-year-old again, riding on his shoulder. It was a strange way to rekindle an old bond. Ours was an act of love and desperation, ultimately futile except for the moment of connection it provided for the two of us. Our temporary partnership depended on Mother being the odd one out, just as the moments of connection I had with her came mostly at my father's expense. Yearning to be on each parent's team, a child is never neutral.

College, marriage, and a career that took me to distant states were convenient excuses to avoid my parents' bitter war. I telephoned and wrote and remembered cards for Easter, but I rarely visited. When I did, I was always struck by Dad's enduring good looks, his full dark hair, his slenderness and health. And his resignation to a marriage that consisted mainly of truces and eruptions.

I called my mother after reading Dad's news, and she supplied a few details. They had been bickering as usual one day and she claimed that he smacked her. Her response: "I don't know why in the hell you don't just leave."

Dad considered for a moment and replied, "You know, I think I will."

He moved into a studio apartment the next week.

During the following months I read his letters and wrote back, and talked to my mother to compare her version of the story to his. For once, they agreed. He visited and took her out to dinner, ran errands and took her to doctor's appointments. It looked to me, from a thousand miles away, as if they were dating again.

Whenever I received a letter from Dad I wrote back immediately, anxious to continue a relationship that I never expected to have with him. I learned to read between the lines, and the stiff formality began to leave his sentences. He confessed that he never meant to take the promised promotion and return to Columbus, a fact that had long been obvious to me. "Mother will never forgive me for not moving back to Ohio," he wrote.

He would never have forgiven himself if he had. Ohio was a snare of family obligations that he escaped by retreating to the wild beaches and mountains of the Pacific Northwest. But his retreat was not to last. He lived on Puget Sound long enough to see his favorite haunts altered beyond recognition by urban sprawl. In our letters we fretted over the loss of all things we held dear—low tides with their abundant clams and oysters, the fragrant mountain forests that seemed endless and pristine. The fishing he could never get enough of, his beloved salmon and steelhead. But over the years his jocular fishing buddies had drifted away. He sold his skiff and neatly organized tackle boxes and hand-shellacked cane rods. He quit going to steelhead club meetings and salmon roasts. Drank more.

A group of old friends talked me into attending my twentieth high school reunion in 1991. I had not seen my parents for nearly five years, and when I called to tell my mother I was coming, she sounded pleased.

She seemed less pleased when I arrived, for my timing intruded on her favorite radio talk show. I should have planned on staying with my best and oldest girlfriend who lived in Seattle. I should have told her I would wait on the front porch until her show was over. But she opened the door and waved me inside and after a brief hug she settled back into her armchair. I went into the bedroom where I had slept for the first eighteen years of my life and lay on my back, tracing with my eye the patterns on the wallpaper. How many afternoons and evenings had I spent in that room, longing for acceptance, direction, and a sense of who I was? There was nothing there for me now except painful memories.

I went into the back yard, amazed by the height and girth of conifers that had once been purchased as live Christmas trees. They formed a shady haven, a reminder of the woods that had once covered the hillside beyond. My love of native plants and wildlife started there, when I began to learn the names of trees and flowers. In early spring, long white panicles draped from Indian plum, shadowed by feathery hemlocks and Pacific yew. Red-flowered currant soon followed. In summer, blackberries grew where enough sunlight reached the ground, and I spent long afternoons there with my mother, filling buckets. Her blackberry pies smelled rich and fragrant as they baked. They tasted like the wilderness.

One September afternoon I arrived home from fourth grade, startled by movement in the woods. The treetops shuddered so violently I braced for an earthquake. But while the trees jerked about, the ground remained at rest. Then, with a burst of black smoke, a bulldozer skidded into view. Jolted by its blade catching on root balls, it lurched across the tangled shreds of a hazelnut tree.

Until that day I did not understand that the friendly couple who had moved away the year before had owned that forest, and now it belonged to someone else. A sense of betrayal seeped around the edges of my shock. The place where I had spent my childhood was being destroyed in front of me. I began to wave my arms and shriek. Used to having kids watch him work, the driver waved and made the big dozer toot like a train whistle as he directed its blade into the blackberry patch.

I ran into the house and slammed my bedroom door. The whine of machinery and the snapping of wood stabbed at me as I lay with a pillow over my head.

Evening brought quiet and I stepped out the back door.

Top left: the author in her favorite madrona, 1960.

Top right: the author, age six, at the beach with her father, 1959.

Right: the author with her mother at Mt. Rainier National Park, 1959.

My heart raced as I ran along the path leading into the woods. An absence loomed ahead, more sky than should appear through the leafy canopy at that time of year. When I saw the slash pile I bolted for it. The vines from which I had gathered inch-long blackberries lay in a tangled heap. Leaves of the uprooted Indian plum hung from their branches like burst balloons. I turned, eyes stinging, and ran headlong up a hillside to a big madrona that leaned far over the bluff above our house. I shinnied along its trunk and stared over the familiar roofs of the neighborhood, the forested ridges beyond, and the slate water of Puget Sound. Hugging the tree, I beat my fist against it until the crown shook. Then I pulled out my pocketknife and began to gouge: "Don't cut the woods down!"

I only partly finished. Frustrated by my clumsy hand and the bald fact of my helplessness, I carved, "Don't cut . . ." and threw the knife to the ground.

My mother was waiting when I slipped back into the house. "You'll be all right," she said as she let me in.

But the truth was, I was never all right after that. The best part of me was gone.

And now I sat looking at all that remained of my childhood playground, companion and instructor—a dozen pines and noble firs that were now so crowded together they formed a screen beyond which I could see none of the houses that replaced my beloved woods.

My mother opened the sliding glass door and told me dinner was ready. To my surprise, I found only one place setting on the dining room table. "Aren't you hungry?" I asked. "You didn't have to cook just for me."

"Here you go," she said as she laid a plate in front of me. "Eat." She took her plate from the kitchen into the small bedroom that my father once used as his office, and ate in front of a television set.

I did what I was told, and ate my dinner. I felt as if no time had passed since I was a girl who wished she had a regular family. Whose mother besides my own would have nothing to say to a daughter she hadn't seen in years? After I left home for college, neither of my parents inquired about my life, my work, or how I was doing. They had not attended my graduation, and the only comment my mother made when I finished graduate school was to ask if she would have to call me Dr. Marsh. They had barely acknowledged the invitation to my wedding in 1984. The strangest thing about all of this was that it seemed normal to me, for I had not expected anything else.

I got up from the table and washed my plate, stirred some cream into a cup of coffee, rinsed the spoon and set it in the dish drainer. Instantly my mother swept into the kitchen to chide me about the way I had placed the spoon.

My father must have known that after a day together my mother and I would be on each other's nerves. The following afternoon he stepped in to rescue me, or perhaps it was my mother he hoped to assist. He nodded me toward his car.

"So . . . where to—South Center?"

I'd been away for twenty years. He no longer knew me well enough to imagine that I might want anything but what I'd wanted as a high school sophomore: to traipse the vacuous corridors of an indoor shopping mall.

"No thanks," I said.

Without further discussion he pointed the station wagon north. Traffic was light on the interstate that morning; a half-hour later, we were sailing down the Dearborn Street off-ramp, and I knew where we were headed. Lunch first, at Ivar's—not the cavernous Acres of Clams but its airy auxiliary, a coffee shop on Elliot Bay with tall windows and blue canvas awnings. Lunch for Dad included two martinis, up and dry, and cigarettes to chase them. "I never inhale," he told me. Slender and fit and scarcely graying at seventy-three, he was so astoundingly resilient I was tempted to believe him. He squinted through the cigarette smoke and regarded me, his only offspring, as if he were looking into a mirror.

After lunch we departed for the Ballard Locks, whose iron gates regulated flow between the tidal bay and the fresh water of Lake Washington. The August sky was a washed haze on the indeterminate cusp between foggy and fair, and it turned the skyline of Seattle to a fading watercolor. The smell of mussels, salt, and creosote rose from the opaque water.

Beside the locks was our destination, the fish ladder, a staircase that might have been described as spiral except the word implies a grace absent from what lay below us, a series of right-angled concrete walls and dark square pools. Thin green curtains of water poured from one square into the next. When I was very young, Dad took me there to watch in wonder as salmon flashed in crowded squads beneath my small, patent-leathered toes.

A sheen of oily water twenty feet below slapped the concrete bulkhead. Dad and I stood in silence, each with our own thoughts.

One of the watery rungs of the fish ladder stirred. A shot of silver wriggled up the curtain into the next square pool, then the next, and the next as the bright torpedo leapt toward our feet. A slender fish, no more than a couple of feet long including the tail. When it reached the final tier I could have touched its moss-green dorsal fin. It vanished into a murky tunnel that ran under the street and I imagined it emerging into the daylight far upstream, swimming south for the Green River and its tributary the Puyallup, to a smaller creek and a smaller one beyond it as the water tumbled from snow still melting high in the Cascades, at last to lay its eggs in a clear and unlogged gravel stream at the base of Mt. Rainier.

Dad and I kept our eyes on the fish ladder. We stood for an hour in the yellow light of late summer as a dozen salmon climbed the ladder and finned away. Cheered to see them, I cheered them on. At last, a fine rain began to wet the concrete. We turned back to the car and drove home.

15

THE BRIDGER-TETON FOREST PLAN was made final in 1990, but resolving an appeal filed by American Rivers required several additional years to complete. The complaint had been that the list of potential Wild and Scenic Rivers included in the plan was inadequate, since it had relied on guidelines that had since been updated. The forest agreed to a complete re-inventory of eligible rivers, and as recreation staff the job fell to me. It took me across the forest with camera and data sheets, to pockets of watery wonder from Big Fall Creek west of the town of LaBarge to the headwaters of the Yellowstone deep in the Teton Wilderness.

I spent a week in the wilderness in an effort to record as many river candidates as could be seen in only a few days. The forks of the upper Buffalo, Pacific and Atlantic Creeks, the upper Snake River, the Thorofare: all worthy to be called Wild Rivers, which indeed they were. But something shifted deep inside me the first time I laid eyes on the headwaters of the Yellowstone.

From the Hawks Rest patrol cabin a sheer stone wall stood on the north side of the river, an inaccessible rampart far above the valley's early morning fog. It narrowed to a jutting point near the boundary between the Teton Wilderness and Yellowstone National Park, a lonesome perch where peregrine falcons made their nests. The cliff face softened with daylight as I followed a game trail beside the river, the silence broken only by a rhythmic sluicing, the slip and slide of flowing water. A few feet away, beyond a violet ribbon of fringed gentian and the silver-green leaves of overhanging willows, ran the upper Yellowstone.

Later that day we would pack our gear and leave Hawks Rest to survey the river's uppermost reach, roughly thirty miles from the snowfields of the Absaroka Range to the boundary of Yellowstone National Park. I would record with notebook and checklist and camera the river's Outstandingly

Remarkable Values as defined by the 1968 Wild and Scenic Rivers Act. I shared my camp with Rebecca, a forester and naturalist whose area of responsibility included the Teton Wilderness. She was there to inspect outfitter camps and trail conditions, and to see what I was up to.

In recognition of the twentieth anniversary of the Wild and Scenic Rivers Act, the Chief of the Forest Service had pledged to expand the number of protected rivers by 20 percent. The Bridger-Teton National Forest held the source not only of the Yellowstone but of the Snake and the Green, rivers of regional and national importance. This was the kind of work that came too rarely for my taste, even for people working for the agency that oversees magnificent backcountry. I stood at the foot of Hawks Rest on that August morning, humbled by the immensity of the wilderness and the majesty of the river, and the task ahead seemed both daunting and superfluous. I wore with great unease my responsibility to record this river properly, not because I doubted its merit. But I had faced this choppy confluence before—the one between my quasi-religious zeal for all things wild and my need to supply objective and persuasive arguments to support my judgments. In addition to passion, I needed credibility, for the Forest Service, elected officials, and various local skeptics wanted facts, not feelings. They wanted answers to such questions as *What is the point?* This reach of the Yellowstone was already protected as part of the Teton Wilderness. Why spend time and money on an inventory if nothing will change after designation? Won't recognition only bring more people? I didn't have the answers yet but I intended to provide them.

At the trailhead Rebecca and I loaded the pack stock with little conversation, bashful strangers preparing to sleep in the same tent for the coming week.

On our first evening at Hawks Rest, twenty-six miles from the trailhead, I stood on the pack bridge to stretch my legs as the Yellowstone slid beneath the hoof-scuffed decking. Downstream, the river meandered in elaborate loops, dawdling over its bed as if resting up for the waterfalls to come. Upstream, the silky strand of water led my gaze past meadows and willows and forests to the crest of the Absarokas. Two great plateaus bounded the glacial valley, narrowing westward to escarpments that mirrored one another. Hawks Rest and Yellowstone Point, twin portals guarding the river's uppermost stronghold. Between the rims of the high plateaus a ruddy alpenglow lit the west face of a singular stone curtain—Thunder Mountain. Though it blocked the view beyond, in the coming days we would see what lay on the far side as we followed the Yellowstone Trail to the river's source.

Getting there was not the effortless ride the contour map had suggested. Miles upstream from Hawks Rest, with Thunder Mountain still rising in the distance, it felt as though the trail as well as the river carried a westward current. We bushwhacked through willow thickets and ran into deadfall, which we cleared with an ax and a crosscut saw. When we left the tangle for the wide skies above a forest that had burned in 1988, I tolerated rather than enjoyed the view. Snag-studded canyons shimmered with heat waves. I slumped in the saddle like a half-empty sack of grain and dreamed about a cool shower and a cold beer. We rode in silence and stared through the shade-free snags of lodgepole pines, and as the sun baked our shoulders it felt as if the fires of '88 might still be burning.

At last we found relief from the sun in a forested gorge. My face was a mask of trail dust blackened by soot, and I was attempting to transfer the worst of the grime onto a bandana when behind me Rebecca shouted.

I twisted around in the saddle as she jabbed a finger to her left. Seeing nothing but darkness under a stand of spruce, I reined Coyote to a reluctant stop, pushed back my hat and took off my sunglasses. Two enormous bull moose stood in the shadows, their antlers nearly touching as the pair of long solemn faces returned my gaze.

My horse Coyote initiated a series of nose jerks to register his impatience and I let him slowly move ahead. Rebecca trotted up behind me a minute later.

"Weren't they gorgeous?"

As if she'd never seen a moose. Recently from the Chugach National Forest, she was used to seeing creatures twice the size of Rocky Mountain moose. Alaska was a vast land inhabited by giants—moose and bears and honker mosquitoes and salmon as long as your leg. With its great chains of mountains and Amazon-scale rivers, Alaska was wild beyond my imagining. When Rebecca arrived at the Buffalo Ranger District I thought she might find the Teton Wilderness small and unremarkable, but she saw at every bend in the trail an echo of the north.

Her enthusiasm and curiosity reminded me of pioneering wildlife ecologist Olaus Murie, who settled in this part of Wyoming after his early years in Alaska because the mountains near Jackson Hole reminded him of the far north. Where else besides Alaska—and the region surrounding

Yellowstone—could one stand on a ridge and see nothing but mountains in all directions and share the trails with moose and grizzly bears? The day before, we had followed Thorofare Creek upstream to its confluence with Open Creek, not far from the spot proclaimed by *Outside* magazine as the most distant point from a road in the lower 48. Like Alaska, this place was a redoubt for vanishing superlatives.

As we rode the Yellowstone Trail I balanced on one stirrup for photographs, vainly trying to keep Coyote's ears out of my pictures. In a spiral notebook I recorded landforms and wildflowers, scenic vistas and textbook examples of the forces of mountain-building and erosion. Riverside willows flashed the signatures of each species. Booth's willow spread upright branches, its leaves already flecked with autumn yellow. A whiplash willow, favored by browsing moose, waved its glossy leaves from ten-foot wands. Wolf willows, compact shrubs with silver-green foliage, hugged a dry channel like a row of porcupines.

I worried over the official Wild and Scenic River inventory form that awaited my attention, a form designed to reduce the wonders of the wild to bloodless data. The most perplexing parts of the evaluation had to do with attributes such as scenery, an essential but subjective value as compared with the presence of endangered species or unique geologic features. The latter were either present or not; who was to say what made scenery outstandingly remarkable? Further, I was supposed to restrict my attention to the river itself and the quarter-mile corridor on each side, but when considered in such a narrow frame, without benefit of context, each stream varied from all the others only in minor detail—the kind of rocks and mix of willows, the intensity of cobalt or aquamarine that settled into the deep, clear pools. A river was more than flowing water. It included everything from the silt-slick bed to the canyon rim a thousand feet above. Perhaps it included the gleam of starlight touching the cured grass on that distant rim.

And as surely as it carried water, the river carried memories, pathways to the human soul, one vital link between ourselves and the wild world which is our native home. Rough stone tools lying near choice campsites reminded us of the antiquity of human habitation in the mountains. In historic times, the earliest fur trappers and mountain men passed this way. The river was the namesake of the world's first national park. I could not divorce this knowledge from the water that passed before me now.

Horse pals taking a break on the trail, Teton Wilderness.

It was mid-afternoon when we reached the foot of Thunder Mountain. We stopped for a late lunch beside Castle Creek, still racing ice-cold and milky at the end of August. I wandered upstream and photographed the pleated drape of hardened lava that was the south face of Thunder Mountain. I photographed the imprints left by aquatic insects in a veneer of wet clay. I was contemplating the fresh grizzly bear tracks in front of me, thinking it was time to turn around, when I jumped at the loud shriek behind me.

Had I flushed the bear off its day bed only to have it stumble into Rebecca and her lunch? Who had the pepper spray? Not me. Another cry, now wild and joyful, and I knew there was no bear. I shouldered through the willows and found Rebecca's Forest Service uniform in a pile beside the river. Shining like a seal, she bounced from the water, laughing with delight.

I slid my hands into the numbing current, overtaken by a pang of yearning. On backpacking trips in my twenties I was the first to shed my clothes and dive into an icy mountain lake. It was a measure of the wildness around me that I never worried that a stranger might happen along and see. It was a measure of the wildness in me. The alpine lakes of long ago gave me a form of baptism, a ritual of savage consummation. But I'd spent the bulk of my life since then cultivating the reserve that now seemed out of place beside the untamed Yellowstone. After three

Cow moose pausing to drink in a beaver pond.

days of riding mainline trails we had yet to meet another party but my self-training had been so complete that even in the farthest reaches of the Teton Wilderness I couldn't put it aside. I watched Rebecca shaking out her damp hair and thought, *That used to be me.*

Rebecca's leap into the river confirmed my early suspicion that this wasn't going to be the standard Forest Service pack trip. The men I worked with were generally more comfortable with the pack stock than they were with people, and a few of them shared the view that the wilderness was no place for a woman.

The sun hung low over the rimrock as we trotted across a meadow to make camp. Released from their cinches and saddle blankets, the horses rolled in the grass and shook like wet dogs. I unfurled the tent beside the river while Rebecca tuned the guitar she'd top-packed across two panniers full of grain.

Shadows filled the tight valley where two small creeks came together a mile upstream from camp. The map named them: the North Fork and South Fork of the Yellowstone River. After we saw to the horses and made camp I took a walk upstream to meet these forks. The canyon walls loomed closer and the forest gave way to krummholz and stringers of fir between converging avalanche chutes.

The trail broke into a meadow and a great wedge of mountain split the river's current. From opposite sides of the wedge two forks joined, north and south: the birthplace of the Yellowstone. I boulder-hopped until I could stand on two rocks, one in each stream. The blue air of evening hovered over the water and shadows climbed the canyon walls. The highest point in the Teton Wilderness, 12,136-foot Younts Peak, cleaved the sky like a bronze ax. In that mountain stronghold, as far as one could be from what we called civilization, where the prattle of water over boulders mixed with the falcon-wing rush of wind on mountaintops, I could have happily taken my final breath.

On my way back to camp I undressed beside a pool. My knees folded and I sank into the water. When I came up, I didn't shriek with exhilaration the way Rebecca had; the shock of the cold took my breath. I staggered to shore and yanked my clothing over wet skin. Skinny-dipping wasn't as fun as it used to be, and with sadness I realized it wasn't the mountain water that had changed.

We washed the dinner dishes and Rebecca opened a battered faux-leather case and pulled out her guitar. There was nowhere to build a campfire without leaving a scar so we went without one as the cold air drained like a long, contented sigh from the snowfields of the Continental Divide. Heavy cast-aluminum panniers, certified bear-resistant, served as seats, and on that chilly night at 8,500 feet they gave new meaning to the term "butt-cold."

The discomfort of chilled backsides was dismissed as the Milky Way threaded a ribbon of stars across the moonless sky as the headwaters of the Yellowstone chattered along with the chords of Rebecca's guitar. She played until her fingers grew numb then passed the guitar to me. We laughed as we tried to remember the lyrics to old folk songs and made them up when we couldn't, a pair of wild women singing to the treetops. Starlight touched the guitar's brass frets, the faint gleam ample substitute for the warmth and snap of a campfire. A pack of coyotes began to yip and we joined them with raucous howls. Rebecca and I were no longer strangers.

The next morning I laid one of the standard Wild and Scenic River inventory forms on a clipboard. The first item to be addressed stared from the page like a jaded postal clerk: "At least one federally listed Threatened or Endangered species (or no fewer than three *species of concern* as identified in the Forest Plan) are present. List species in the space below."

This one was a no-brainer, a good way to limber up for the more difficult questions ahead. The return of wolves to Yellowstone was a few years in the future, but every other critter that had inhabited the Yellowstone region when Lewis and Clark passed through still thrived. Peregrine falcon, I wrote. Whooping crane, though none had been seen since the one that spent a few days near Hawks Rest two years before. Bald eagle, grizzly bear. The form gave no space for more.

Next. "Evidence of human influence on natural processes minimal."

Another easy one. There were a few Canada thistle patches and some of the outfitters were still using salt blocks to bait elk out of Yellowstone National Park, but the hoof prints we left in the trail the day before were already covered by the tracks of bears, moose, and cranes. The night sky had been a cascade of stars pouring their distant light across a black canvas. The silence was deep, stretching from rim to canyon rim and farther back in time than could be imagined.

Next question. "Scenic quality outstanding for __ miles of river segment (must exceed 50 percent)."

Scenery: that poor cousin of beauty. Unaltered land held an innate harmony, its colors, forms, and lines responding to the ancient dictates of geology, the softening influence of plants and weather. The elegant patterns and arrangements expressed by the wild earth informed our notions of aesthetics. Such land inspired an ineffable sense of awe and wonder, a connection with the divine. This is what I thought of as beauty. *Scenery* brought to mind a barely-glanced-at backdrop, most frequently observed from the window of a speeding automobile. "Isn't that pretty," people would remark at national park overlooks, just before collecting their kids and moving on. This canyon did not abide a brief, distracted glance or the kind of impatient shuffling that one saw at Old Faithful as the crowd waited, only to disperse before the geyser finished its eruption. You had to plan ahead, you had to work, to reach this remote quarter, and you had to assume an uncommonly slow pace, for even the Buffalo District's team of fox-trotter mules needed more than one day to reach the birthplace of the Yellowstone. *Scenic* was not the word I needed. The upper Yellowstone River was a place infused with power, not painted-on prettiness. It was the home of beauty and all that it implied—magnificence, splendor, evidence of the numinous. On those mountains, on those boulders in the river, were the fingerprints of God.

There wasn't room on the form to write all of that; instead I jotted *28 miles (100 percent)*.

Headwaters of the Yellowstone River and Younts Peak, highest point in the Teton Wilderness, 1990.

I quickly dispatched the remaining items, giving each Outstandingly Remarkable Value the highest rating possible. I imagined calling Rebecca over to announce, "Hey, look here. I finished filling out this form, and guess what—the river is a nine." She would nod, gaze past me with a vague and secret smile, and go back to playing her guitar.

I put the clipboard away and unfolded a topographic map. As I pressed the sheet flat across the panniers Rebecca appeared like a moth to a flame. Our eager fingertips traced the trails we had ridden and the high divide to come. We pointed to the place where we had seen the two bull moose, the meadow from which we listened to sandhill cranes and bugling elk. The map burst open with stories, recording our journey in the language of the land. It delivered memories, images, the earthy scent of pond water and the bite of wild chives. Like my inventory form, it was only a sheet of paper covered with symbols that represented factual information—elevations, geographic features. Why did it hold us so?

The Woodard Canyon Trail wound among massive spruce trees whose silver trunks stood like pillars in the mist. The quiet was as dense as the fog and it felt is though I could reach out and grab both. The silence of deep wilderness absorbed our intermittent talk, the soft percussion of

Ferry Lake near the Continental Divide, Teton Wilderness, 1990.

horse farts, the scrape of steel-shod hooves against boulders in the trail. We climbed into a cloud suffused with light. Rebecca kept pointing to things that enchanted her—crimson paintbrush glowing like a bouquet of highway flares, a milky cascade emerging from a blush of rosy *Mimulus*, our horses' breath mixing with the fog.

Above the spruce forest the high country opened like unfolding hands. Bright shoals of buttercups hemmed late snow banks. We rode onto the snow and followed bear tracks over the spine of the great divide. We stopped for a break in a sheltered notch and stared across the miles of alpine tundra to the south. As the clouds began to lift and break apart, dabs of sunlight slid across the Buffalo Plateau. I gazed into the gorge ahead—the South Fork of the Buffalo, where we would camp that night. When I turned to say something to Rebecca she was putting on her raincoat.

"I won't be long," she said, and strode away.

The stock stood with their ample haunches to the wind, tied with what I knew were secure hitches to a stand of dwarf subalpine fir. Deceptively placid with half-closed eyes and ears set back at an angle of apparent inattention, each horse rested his left hind leg on the leading edge of the hoof as if planning to settle in for a good long nap. But I knew that if I followed Rebecca they would start working the hitches loose and if they managed it I'd see them again at the trailhead. Duty prevailed over desire and I contented myself with a seat on a rocky knob beside the horses. The trail was a thin brown strand in a sea of emerald green that followed the dips and bulges of the plateau until it disappeared over Marston Pass. Rebecca was a small moving speck in the distance.

Rebecca was one of those shafts of sunlight pouring through the dusty window of my Forest Service career. I'd spent most of it attempting to meet the unspoken requirement that I conduct myself in ways considered appropriate for a federal agency manager. This did not include wild laughter, howling with coyotes, or leaving my green uniform in a heap beside the river. With my peers I practiced the art of dispassionate rationality, contented for the most part to record my "specialist input" in the artless terms that belonged on an inventory form. But for a week in the wilderness, Rebecca and I had been ourselves, no apologies required. I realized that we both had trained to be two people, the wild and the tamed, balanced precariously on opposing boulders, a foot in each stream.

We were not alone. In the woods my colleagues, men and woman alike, would loosen up and reveal odd secrets, sharing glimmers of untrammeled humanity.

Months after the Yellowstone River survey, I labored over my final report, trying to assemble all I had experienced on that pack trip back in August, to describe it in terms germane to the Wild and Scenic Rivers Act. *Outstanding* had hardly been in question the evening I straddled the forks of the Yellowstone as the sunset burnished Younts Peak. But the Yellowstone was, at that far reach, only a little creek, murmuring over its cobbles as did hundreds of other streams in northwestern Wyoming. I would have trouble arguing with anyone who claimed it was merely typical. In this part of the world, outstanding and typical were one and the same.

I struggled for objectivity, playing down my personal enchantment with the Yellowstone until my report began to read like a description of the physical properties of gold. Such qualities as softness, malleability, and specific gravity described the metal but did not hint at the reasons it was so highly prized. Likewise the river: sterile descriptions told nothing of the way I had experienced it. Bear tracks, bull moose, and the sound of wind in the rimrock were more to the point. I abandoned the computer and walked for an hour to revive my enthusiasm.

When I returned to my desk I sorted through my field notes. A topographic map slid from the leaves of inventory forms, and as I unfolded it a particle of sand from the Yellowstone River fell into my hand. Translucent, pale amber, and roughly round, it gathered and held the November light

Canyon of Whetstone Creek in the Teton Wilderness, which Olaus Murie referred to as his "place of enchantment."

like a tiny sun. I rolled the fragment in my palm. I put it in my mouth and swallowed.

The sand grain must have triggered my ability to work. I wrote for the rest of the afternoon, editing only to make my statements clear, not to question or dilute their implications. At last I felt satisfied. By describing the upper Yellowstone as completely and accurately as possible, I found that without trying I had addressed the skeptics' questions and portrayed a river that exemplified what was meant by *outstandingly remarkable*.

I pressed flat the map's creases and my finger traced the egg-blue line that meandered toward the Continental Divide. On the page the Yellowstone curved beyond Hawks Rest and Thunder Mountain to the ice-cold water tumbling from Younts Peak like a wild child running down a set of stairs. The fluorescent light over my desk faded to a moonless night in August. Frost gathered on the meadow grass as Rebecca played her guitar, laughing between forgotten, invented, and finally remembered lyrics. Singing to the coyotes and the Milky Way, we lingered late, our music mixing with the horses' bells and the gentle slap of the rising Yellowstone, before it drifted into the night.

16

FAR FROM THE TETON WILDERNESS stand the southern ranges of the Bridger-Teton National Forest: Mahogany Ridge, Commissary Ridge, the Tunp Range, and Porcupine Ridge, each cloaked in aspen and conifer where water collects and stays all summer, while the dry exposed aspects burst with seasonal wildflowers. At the turn of the twentieth century, as many as three hundred thousand ewes and lambs trailed each summer over a narrow col in those mountains northeast of Cokeville, Wyoming, where the Salt River Range steps down into the limestone and quartzite hogbacks of Commissary Ridge. The flowered gap between the headwaters of LaBarge and Spring Creeks became known as Sheep Pass.

In the 1880s, a blink of geologic time ago, Sheep Pass was a pristine and prehistoric defile between wild mountains, remote from human settlement at nearly ten thousand feet. Snow lay deep on its north-facing flank and an explosion of wildflowers burst from the damp red clay when the cornices finally melted toward the end of July. Part of the unclaimed west, it was public domain and free for the taking. Villages in Star Valley, the upper Bear River, and the Green River Basin were young and rough-hewn, slow to prosper in their snow-bound isolation. Livestock grazing was one enterprise that brought income. But by 1900 huge sheep operations from out of state began to compete with the locals for the summer range and Sheep Pass belonged to the man who got there first. As with the various rushes for western gold, the only incentive was to push the season and use as much as you could before somebody else laid claim to what you wanted—in this case the lush high-elevation wildflower parks. Within a decade the ungrazed basins of the Commissary, Salt River Range, and southern Wyoming Range were gone. The competition only grew more fierce, and by the turn of the twentieth century the cattlemen were pushing back from northern ranges that they'd claimed in the Green River and

View north from Sheep Pass, Salt River Range, Wyoming, 1999.

Hoback Basins. Ridges were declared "deadlines" beyond which sheep ranchers risked the loss of both herds and herders if they dared to trespass on range the cattlemen considered theirs.

In 1905 the Yellowstone Forest Reserve was expanded to include what later became the Bridger National Forest. Domestic livestock grazing came under an allotment system and the number of cattle or sheep was limited to what was allowed under each rancher's permit, a system intended to match the number and distribution of livestock with what the land could support. By then much of the damage had been done.

The Sheep Pass trail begins at an unmarked curve along a gravel forest road in the upper Smiths Fork. The trail is a steep two miles to a spectacular view. One September day in 1995 I went to Sheep Pass as part of a group of Forest Service managers to look at the range conditions, past efforts to restore some of its former splendor, and to discuss what we might do to help it along. No range management expert, I was there because I knew the trail and because I wished to learn from those who saw what I could not in the flower-dabbed meadows that looked natural to the casual observer. Along with the forest supervisor, district ranger, and an assortment of Forest Service and Game and Fish range and wildlife experts, we had the company of Alma Winward, renowned plant ecologist from the regional office in Ogden. And Leon, a lifelong sheep rancher from the Spanish Pyrenees, who held the grazing permit for this part of the forest.

Part of my job was to photograph evidence of the land's recovery since the Sheep Pass livestock driveway was closed and check dams were placed in the raw, eroding gullies. Judith, the range conservationist in charge of that allotment, kicked off our discussion by unfolding a yellowed, weather-beaten map across the hood of her green Forest Service truck. The map displayed a network of historic trails and sheep driveways. Driveways, not in the sense of paved spurs to suburban garages, but referring to the narrow ridgetop routes the herders used to drive their bands of several thousand from one subalpine basin to another until the season ended not long after Labor Day. On Judith's map thick red lines ran along the ridges and over high divides like arteries on an anatomical chart. And arteries they were, from which the bands that grazed this summer range dispersed into the flowered basins from Sheep Pass into the forks of Spring Creek and Corral Creek, miles to the north.

The Sheep Pass driveway was closed for good in 1969 and after that the sheep arrived around the end of June by truck.

Leon, whose band of seven hundred ewes grazed near Sheep Pass, immigrated to Wyoming when he was twenty. With a wide sweep of his arm he indicated the clouds of dust that once hung over the driveway in September, dust that did not settle for days as the sheep trailed, one band behind the other, over Sheep Pass and out the Smiths Fork.

"Summer in the mountains was short," he said. "The grazing season was over by the first of September and the sheep had to trail over snow in July."

It made me wonder how it could be worthwhile trailing sheep from far out on the desert basins to summer in the high passes of the Salt Rivers for what amounted to two months' feed. But—what feed it was. For sheep, the wildflower parks in the Salt River Range were the equivalent of a Häagen-Dazs stand, where they ate nonstop from July to September.

As he gazed up the mountainside, Leon cut a regal profile in his black silk scarf and blue plaid Pendleton shirt, his jeans weathered to the contours of his legs, leather bota bag on his hip.

"Grape juice?" he offered with a grin, and sipped his Spanish wine. He reminisced about his many summers herding sheep when this land was used for little besides grazing. No mineral wealth lay underground and most of the timber still stood uncut. Weekend campers had not yet discovered the remote backcountry far to the south of Yellowstone. It belonged to the sheepmen.

Their ghosts shadowed me everywhere I hiked in the mountains north of Sheep Pass. On aspen trunks their names were inscribed, some with hometowns, many with dates. I found inscriptions carved by men who herded here before I was born: Humberto Garcia, 1945. Valor Lealtad, 1950. Billy Mumford, 1937. The last, a local, I surmised from the Anglo name and the creek named Mumford not far away. On another tree, a more intriguing inscription: Ruth Ward Mumford, 1937. The lone female name gazed unblinking from a ridgetop grove across the decades since she carved it. What was her life like, riding the summer range with Billy, keeping camp and herding woolies, closing her eyes every night on the blizzard of stars that hung over the Salt River Range? It might have seemed ordinary to her, a routine of hard work that began every day before dawn. But she left a carefully carved message on an aspen that said *This was not ordinary*. I believed her.

Some of the tree carvings were testaments to loneliness. I found a grove of aspens where Mexican camp tenders had engraved cartoon palm trees into the trunks to make their camps look more like home. Their images of women's torsos, most without faces or heads, were like two-dimensional mannequins, modestly covered with panties and brassieres.

Along one driveway, the outline of a brassiere was carved six feet up an aspen trunk, with no accompanying body. At first glance, it looked as if the tree was wearing sunglasses. Perhaps the artist was interrupted when a bear tore into his frying tortillas. Perhaps he was imagining the brassiere flung off in a moment of passionate abandon. That is how it looked to me, its straps curving around the tree where it was carelessly tossed some sixty years before.

Objects of lonely lust, the women and their undergarments weathered into aspen bark and slowly became part of it. Each year a few more of the old trees fell, taking their inscriptions back to earth. No half-hearted graffiti, the carvings were artistically rendered with careful script and neat lettering in block or script.

The scabby letters standing out from a pale aspen canvas whetted my imagination. They made me want to look up Ruth Ward Mumford and ask her to tell me stories of 1937.

As it happened, I wrote a story about this inscription for a local magazine, and not long after it was published I received a letter from her son, a retired medical doctor in his eighties with a return address of Alpine, Wyoming. He had this to offer about his mother's history: "Ruth had taken me, age 6 in 1928, to Cambridge, Mass where she was attending Massachusetts Institute of Technology on scholarship. She ultimately received her Master's Degree at University of Michigan Ann Arbor and worked extensively in the field of public health and nursing education. She became Director of Child Health in the state of Utah and passed away in 1977."

In spite of the romance of their fanciful tree carvings, the early herders left their mark on the driveways as well as on the trees. The day our group of resource managers visited, the red shale at Sheep Pass still lay damp the first week of September from recently melted snow. Lupine and mountain willowherb bloomed in scattered clumps, but mostly the ground was bare.

Judith stood on the pass and held a photograph taken in 1979, the year the Forest Service tried to check the mud hemorrhages that bled down the north slope into Spring Creek. The photo showed newly cut logs and branches jammed into the gullies to slow runoff and gather soil. Our group peered down from the pass and I photographed the same logs, now silver

A Peruvian sheepherder's inscription on an aspen trunk. "One year—no more," he wrote.

with age. Although Sheep Pass still ran raw with snowmelt every summer, the check dams were doing their job gathering silt. The slope below us was more green than bare and a stand of lupine was visible as a purple smudge where the twenty-year-old photograph showed only exposed earth.

Alma Winward, who lent his ecological expertise to national forests in Utah, Nevada, and parts of Idaho and Wyoming, explained what happened here. He directed our attention to a stunted pine on a pedestal of earth. It looked as if it had been dropped there by a landscaper's tree spade.

He swept his arm along an imaginary line from the top of the tree's exposed roots. Five feet of soil was missing from under his flattened palm. The driveway had been closed for forty years, but Sheep Pass looked little different from the grainy photograph Judith held up for comparison. The pine bore silent witness to what could never be repaired.

Alma's eyes flashed from a sunburst of creases when he smiled. A youthful-looking sixty, perennially tanned under a broad-brimmed stockman's hat, he smiled often. He named the many species that once cloaked Sheep Pass, a constellation of extravagant bloom. His years as a university professor showed in his patient explanations and a tendency to ask for our conclusions based on what we saw. But he was no urban academic; he grew up in southeastern Idaho and understood the challenges of farming and ranching in harsh country. He tipped his dented hat in the direction he wanted us to look.

Tufted bunchgrass, sulfur buckwheat, and yarrow grew on the long south-facing slope. Backlit by the late summer sun, the curing plants ran in golden waves toward ridges fading into the horizon. What could be more beautiful, I thought—the scene looked as natural as the day the mountains were born.

Alma quickly dispelled my illusion. "All of that should be tall forb," he said.

"Tall forb" is an ecologist's term for a diverse, self-sustaining community of herbaceous perennials that grow only under specific conditions of elevation, aspect, moisture, and soil. *Forb*—because aside from a few attendant species of grass and sedge, these are broad-leafed flowering plants. *Tall*—because the signature species of this ecotype can grow higher than a man.

Someone in the group asked Alma how he could tell the sun-bronzed grassland was out of place. He turned the question back to us, for we'd seen the evidence ourselves: the high elevation; the aspect; the fine-grained soil that could hold June's rain and snowfall for the dry weeks of late summer; the trace remaining of the former ground level now eroded from the pine.

"I always look for a few remnant species hanging on—that tells you a lot." Alma paused, his mind revisiting the decades and vast geography of his experience, conjuring a scene that only he could see. "Geranium has just started to come back on the Wasatch Plateau. It's taken sixty years."

Somehow he found hope in that bleak fact. Wild geranium added organic nutrients, builders of new soil, inviting other plants to find their way home. I wondered at his cheerful optimism. Earlier in the day he had mentioned that in these mountains soil formed at a rate of an inch per thousand years. Was it possible that the soil of sixty thousand years had been beaten away by scrambling hooves in little more than a decade?

The ecologist who chose as his life's purpose the recovery of high-elevation plant communities would have one certain job requirement: patience.

In addition to the perennial barley planted as a temporary fix, wild lupine was beginning to colonize Sheep Pass. Lupine, a member of the pea family and related to crazyweed, was one plant that Leon wanted his sheep to avoid because of its neurotoxins. But Alma said it restored nitrogen to the nutrient-poor soil. I listened to the relative value of lupine discussed between them—good plant, bad plant, depending on your point of view. Good, as long as it was not the only thing growing, they finally agreed. I was glad to see any plants at all.

"It will never come back," said Leon, sadly shaking his head.

"Someday. You helped plant the barley," Alma said. He squinted from under his creased felt hat.

"You need to help, you need to have hope," Leon said. "When I first came to this country I was shocked by the practices. They would never treat the land that way in the Pyrenees. But here—that was how everybody did it in those days."

"Judith tells me you are kind to the land," said Alma.

Leon shrugged in reply. "I'm just an old sheepherder."

He had said that a dozen times that day but his modesty could not deny the intimate knowledge of the mountains in his eyes. I asked questions, wanting to know about his life here. I imagined him a grandfather, with his graying hair and long European face and sparkling eyes, his neck tanned the color of saddle leather. He was a successful businessman, not "just" an old sheepherder. He owned the sheep and the deeded base property and hired a number of herders. I saw his satisfaction with the life he made for himself and his family in this spectacular mountain country.

"My younger son is getting married," he told us over lunch. "Then he is moving back to Spain." Generations swapping continents, his son believed he could make a better go of raising sheep in the Pyrenees.

"Maybe now, he can," Leon gazed into the distance, where the haze of late summer blued the horizon beyond Commissary Ridge. "People want fine wool, not the coarse fiber of my Columbias. Merino sheep can't survive in this climate."

I mentioned the band I saw while driving to the trailhead. Milling along the Smiths Fork were at least a thousand sheep, shoulder to shoulder like rounded concrete riprap and spilling from the mountainside fat as ticks.

"The range must be healthy to produce such rotund sheep."

He agreed. "It has been a wet year. The sheep have done well."

Although Leon's sheep were coming off the summer ranges fattened, the forage was not abundant every year. The cost of doing business was more than the sale of the lambs recovered. The forest roads, much increased and improved since Leon began herding sheep, brought more people seeking backcountry recreation, not encounters with sheep. Men like Leon faced the twilight of a way of life. When the thick old aspens fell, with their names and dates and passionately flung brassieres, the new trees would bear no inscriptions to mark the passing of that history.

"Maybe your grandsons will come back here to raise their sheep," I offered.

He laughed. "Maybe. What do I know? I'm just an old sheepherder."

"It's hard to put a value on this, isn't it?" Alma asked with an arm-sweep toward the mountain slope below us. "I don't know if there's an answer.

"When settlers first came into the mountains they were like us—they found a use for everything and gave it value according to its use. Forests were good for timber and firewood, grasslands good for grazing. Perhaps the purpose of the tall forb community was simply to be beautiful."

The many-colored blooms, the jungle of broad leaves—what better purpose for such plants than to offer us their beauty? A beauty that still thrives in some subalpine basins where sheep and elk nibble flower heads, the sheep now a tenth the number that once moved across the high cirques. Some basins, including Swift Creek just east of the town of Afton, was on a list of potential research natural areas because of the quality of its tall forb community.

Looking out from Sheep Pass, I could easily imagine it as the frontier, the way I often did on the trail to the Burning Bush. The tilted limestone cliffs of the Salt River Range rippled away to the north. Commissary Ridge lay darkly timbered to the south. I could stand there and believe the grass had always tossed in the wind as it did on that September afternoon. A herd of buffalo might have appeared at any moment.

On the trail back to our vehicles Alma spotted a daisy growing from bare limestone. Its flowers spread an inch across, pale violet with golden central discs. He sat on his heels beside it and gently cupped it in his hand. With reverence he said its name—*Erigeron speciosus*—a wildflower nearly eliminated from a mountainside where it had once been common. He told us about the journals kept by early flock masters.

"It must have been something," he said as he straightened. "On the Wasatch Top they unloaded the bands in June, a thousand at a time. The only way they found them later was to watch for the flower heads quivering."

I stared down the draw from where the daisy bloomed and in my imagination saw a garland of it hugging the boulders of that ephemeral

Showy daisy, *Erigeron speciosus.*

creek for as far as I could see. A forest of leafy herbs grew beyond: sticky geranium, tall larkspur, silver lupine, nettle-leaf horse mint, fernleaf lovage, bracted lousewort, leafy Jacob's ladder, sweet cicely, tobacco root, mountain coneflower, meadow rue, Engelmann aster, Rocky Mountain groundsel, western sweet vetch, yellow hawkweed, little sunflower, western valerian, Colorado columbine, sulfur paintbrush, Jessica stick-seed. What blooming extravagance the early herders must have encountered as they carved their names on aspen trees from here north to the Hoback River. They recorded their migrations across the broad cirque basins of the Salt River Range, up one side of the mountains and down the other, until the frosts of September turned the forbs yellow, brittle and dry. Then the flocks climbed Sheep Pass again, raising their clouds of dust, leaving the empty flower stalks to rattle in the autumn wind.

Alma left us that day with a plan for how to help Sheep Pass. Adding to the check dams in deep gullies would catch runoff and give young plants a place to grow and we could gather local seeds from the area and plant them where they would not wash away. We knew we would never see the wildflower parks of old, but each of us resolved to do our part to help the scars heal, not for the next generation but for one in a more distant future. Beyond his knowledge of ecology, Alma left us with the gift of his

Dr. Alma Winward and range monitoring crew measuring plant vigor after a prescribed burn for big game winter range. Gannett Hills, Wyoming, 1996.

enthusiasm. A reminder of why—despite our frustrations about working for the government, driving a green rig in Sagebrush Rebel country, and the sometimes doubtful outcome of our efforts—each of us had chosen a life outdoors, working in a national forest.

Ten years after I stood on Sheep Pass, I assisted in placing a new rangeland analysis transect in a vacant sheep allotment where Leon's band had once grazed. In the intervening years I had learned enough from Alma Winward and other plant ecologists to offer help in reading complex transects that took more than a day to complete. We explored a long ridge running parallel to the North Fork of Murphy Creek, along the east slope of the Salt River Range, where the old sheep driveway, now a recreation trail, passed fields of mule's ear and cutleaf balsamroot, aspen groves and forests of pine and fir. For decades the clamor of ovine bawls and bells rose from the North Fork Basin, but in 1997 the mountains fell into quiet repose. Without the sheep, those hills seemed empty as a vacant building, a concert hall after the last long note had fallen still. I did not expect to miss the woolies, now that they were gone.

Leon had retired and relinquished his permit here. Normally, when a grazing permit is waived back to the US government, a new one is issued to the purchaser of the business. This time, by Leon's request and made possible by the Rocky Mountain Elk Foundation, the Forest Service withdrew the allotment to make it a wildlife sanctuary and forage reserve.

That part of the Salt River Range had long been known as a prime calving ground for elk. Pregnant cows followed the snowline as it receded from the valleys where they spent the winter, arriving in the North Fork of Murphy Creek in May. The calves were old enough to run with the herd by the time the sheep arrived. But Leon said when he retired, "I have hardly used that area the past few years. It belongs to the elk."

The Salt River Range, still deep in winter's snow, towered over a land of long-standing multiple use. In the North Fork, the remnants of sheepherder camps lay silent in the shadows: salt troughs hand hewn from logs, clusters of stakes for tents. The aspens were carved with the usual names and artwork, inscribed with dates going back to the 1920s. Ruth Ward and Billy Mumford's were among them.

Elk had used that country for longer than the earliest sheepherders. Bones and shed antlers washed out of creek gravel, amber-colored and mossy with age. Elk trails were beaten deep into the moist earth, traversing brushy slopes and forests or running straight up the steepest mountainsides.

A reclaimed timber road snaked along beside the creek, its culverts pulled, spring water carving gullies down its center. Intermediate wheatgrass, an introduced species with an odd blue cast, waved chin-high from the old roadbed. Seismic crews camped in the area during the early 1980s as they explored for oil and gas. Cattle still grazed the lower reaches, and sheep still bawled from nearby allotments. Dust rose from the main road as fishermen and picnickers arrived at Murphy Lakes. A line of plastic diamonds along the ridge guided snowmobiles in winter and the old sheep driveway had become a popular trail for ATV riders in the summer.

Here we used the land, but now we had given it back. The oil companies came and found nothing. The timber companies came and cut a handful of trees, planted wheatgrass on the roadbed, and left. The sheep came, drifted around the high basins for the two-month summers, and left with the first snows of September. This pocket of wild country, far from the crowds of Jackson Hole, was left for the elk. As Leon said, it belonged to them.

By 2005, aspen shoots surrounded the stands where sheepherder art and inscriptions decorated the old trees. Ten of us, representing the

Installing a new range monitoring transect, North Fork Murphy Creek, Salt River Range, 2005.

Wyoming Game and Fish Department as well as the Forest Service, along with Alma Winward, set out on a hot July morning to find a place suitable for a "rooted nested frequency transect" in a recovering tall forb park. To conduct this kind of transect it is necessary to record every herbaceous plant within a square meter—even the shriveled stems of early bloomers that wither by the end of June—and repeat the measurement every five feet along a belt one hundred feet long. A complete transect consists of five hundred-foot belts, or one hundred square meters sampled. It's also necessary to have at least two people per team, one to identify the plants and the other to record them as each species is called out. The process, especially on a hot, windless day when the horseflies are numerous, can be lengthy, tedious, and painstaking. As a result, practitioners have developed shorthand, most often using the first two letters of the genus and species name. *Polygonum douglasii* thus becomes PODO. In some cases, diagnostic features replace the multi-syllabic botanical names. *Galium bifolium* (GABI), a tiny relative of bedstraw that is dried to a brown thread by the end of July, can be identified by its twinned fruit capsules that resemble minute fuzzy globes. These are known as monkey balls.

We found a site near the top of the ridge and set to work on the transect after a quick lunch, and as we worked I could hear the occasional

17

After a few years in Jackson Hole, I found that my prediction that I would not return to Montana had largely come true. To people in Bozeman, *The Park* was Yellowstone. In Jackson, the same phrase meant Grand Teton. I found myself longing for the northern ranges of Yellowstone, where I had driven many times on my way to Cooke City and the wedge of Gallatin National Forest that surrounded it. I perused the catalogue of courses offered by the Yellowstone Institute and signed up for one called "Finding your voice in Yellowstone," a hybrid of writing, hiking, and touring the lesser-known places along the roads. The timing, late August, was not one I would have chosen, for the summer crowds would still be present and I had my doubts about finding any little-known spots near a park road.

Arriving at Mammoth Terraces, all I could see from the back of the twelve-passenger van were row after row of parked cars. We made slow-motion circles around the lanes as if on a carnival ride losing power, its orbit in decay along with our hopes of ever finding a free space. There must have been a thousand vehicles baking on the hot asphalt and four times that number of people milling on the boardwalks beyond.

The travertine terraces at Mammoth gleamed like a cave turned inside out, limp stalactites hanging over the edges in dripping, twisted rags. Dead pines cast skeletal lines across the bone-white swells of stone, offering no shade from the ninety-degree heat. Venturing out there on that August afternoon was beyond consideration; it would have been like walking down the handle of a skillet.

The air-conditioned Yellowstone Institute van was a cool capsule of quiet but when we finally found a parking slip we joined the jostling crowds. A baby's cries were drowned by the rattle of a garbage truck lifting a bear-resistant Dumpster while an errant car alarm bayed urgently—beep-beep-beep! Vehicles idled with windows open and radios cranked up. A father shouted orders to his brood as he lined them up for a photo in front of the terraces. Another car alarm began to bleat, this one punctuated with wild whoops and siren bursts. Irony floated like an overheard joke: this was a national park, the nation's flagship park, two million acres of wilderness in the far corner of Wyoming. Visitors came for wildlife, scenery, and memorable outdoor experiences, but most of what lay in front of me could have been replicated in front of a suburban Wal-Mart.

Yet the people strolling the boardwalks seemed to be enjoying themselves. A shorts-clad tourist showed no perturbation from purses and elbows bumping him as he panned the terraces with a video camera. Young men crowded around an idling diesel pickup and agreeably shouted into the driver's open window and at each other. I lectured myself: Americans were enjoying their national park and I should have been glad, however noisy the result. I should have been content to know that attractions like Mammoth and Old Faithful drew most of the people and kept them entertained so solitude-seekers could still find quiet in the backcountry.

On the previous evening, Deborah, our guide and workshop leader, told us about a "secret quiet place" she knew at Mammoth. No one believed this could be possible, and half of us argued for skipping the hour-long drive and holing up in the Lamar Valley where we could write in comparative isolation. Outvoted, I fell into line with my fellow students and tried not to be annoyed with Deborah for hauling us off to Bedlam.

We followed the trace of an abandoned railroad grade into a stand of Douglas fir. The only sign that a narrow-gauge railroad had once delivered tourists to the upper terraces at Mammoth was a grassy bevel in the hillside, now a faint trail. Littered with deer pellets and fallen pinecones, it led apparently nowhere. But nowhere sounded like a great place to go, away from the teeming boardwalks and parking lots and roads. Slowly we lost the sound of RVs chugging up the grade toward Obsidian Cliff, and before I was fully aware of it, our group of twelve was alone. Beside us lay a brass-stained terrace, a pool that gently simmered like a pot of stew. It was twenty degrees cooler under the trees than in the parking lot, and the sweet, spicy scent of sun striking the boughs of Douglas fir filled the air. It took all of ten minutes to get away from the crowds.

The quiet, how it blessed me.

We assembled around Deborah, conceding that she had been right about this secret quiet place. Her pale gray eyes flashed merrily as she prepared us for an afternoon of solo time. Most of us were already scanning the deer trails that led in all directions, eager to started filling the pages in our notebooks.

"See you back here at four o'clock," she said. She glanced at her watch, tossed a long silver braid over her shoulder, and strode away.

We dispersed, off to find our voices. Deborah claimed a patch of fawn-colored sand where she sat cross-legged in baggy purple pants, her pencil scratching purposefully across the page. I selected a direction and wandered until I was drawn to a shaded rock outcrop, a bald dome of charcoal-gray rising like a fossil eggshell from a stand of stunted lodgepole pine. There a spring exhaled hydrogen sulfide, its lobe of travertine wrapping the clearing with stone the color of living flesh. I pressed my hand against the firm young rock and felt it pushing back. The quiet and containment there enveloped me, as though I'd walked into a private room and closed the door.

Sheets of water flowed from the lip of the terrace and plinked onto an entablature of hollow stone. The hot spring breathed and sputtered, gargled and sang. Before I started to write anything, I sat and listened.

Our class had spent the previous afternoon in an exercise of listening. Blindfolded, our eyesight voluntarily eclipsed, we practiced unaccustomed ways of seeing. We learned how hard it was to tell the whisper of a creek from the sough of wind in the trees, and how important it was to know the difference to avoid getting lost or wet. At the end of the day, we gladly yanked off our blindfolds. One member of the group exclaimed, "I can't imagine being blind in Yellowstone. There is so much to see!"

Now at the secret place that Deborah called Narrow Gauge, I closed my eyes and imagined being blind in Yellowstone. It didn't seem so bad. I plugged my senses into the current of rich and varied scents, the freshness of the air. And most of all, the quiet.

Sightlessness for the sighted can be a brief vacation from habitual watching, eyes always on the distant, the next-to-come. Far vistas pull our thoughts ahead as we wait for tomorrow and plan what we'll do next. Our culture praises this trait—we call it vision, foresight. But it is also a distraction from the present moment. For a few minutes at Narrow Gauge my vision was suspended in favor of the here and now, where sun poured warmth onto my arm and shade cast by a heavy branch lay cool across my chest. Eyes closed, I noticed the difference. Sulfurous fumes gathered and dispersed, and I registered their changing intensity. A red-breasted nuthatch called, a soft alto monotone. Beep-beep-beep—it reminded me

Mammoth Terraces, Yellowstone National Park.

of that cursed car alarm, but only superficially. Unlike the alarm the bird's call was gentle and soothing, a natural sound belonging to that place. A hundred feet away I would not have heard it at all.

Quiet invaded my chest and my breathing matched the cadence of the nuthatch call, the water's plink, the inhale-exhale of wind moving through the trees. I wasn't used to such peace, and the contrary part of my brain immediately kicked in, distracting me with an internal clamor that rivaled that of the parking lot. I thought first of the bleating car alarm, evoked by the nuthatch, and of all the car alarms that added to the cacophony of downtown Jackson in the summer. I thought about the tourists milling on the far side of the woods and wondered over the fact that no one else had found this sheltered place.

I think that even if people knew about it they wouldn't come, for there was no marked trail and it certainly wasn't among the park's main attractions. The people I saw on the Mammoth boardwalks inched along in tight clusters, gripping their children's arms with firm hands as they stared into ice-blue pools hot enough to peel away their skin. It was a good thing they stuck to the developed attractions designed to accommodate them, that they didn't go running madcap over brittle crusts of travertine only to fall through and scald their toes. But two thoughts struck me, both with equal force: that they were missing something sublime here, and that they would not have especially enjoyed it.

This line of thought led to a remembered visit from an old Seattle friend. When I asked how she'd slept she shook her head.

"Lousy," she said. "It was too quiet."

She must have felt that disorienting absence of the familiar—even if it consisted of freeway traffic and sirens and garbage trucks at four in the morning. Reassuring sounds, like a wind-up clock ticking in a new puppy's bed.

Giving my thoughts a gentle shove back to the immediate moment in Yellowstone, I recalled a recent weekend spent in a campground full of RVs. At dinnertime a chorus of diesel generators drowned out a nearby waterfall, but at ten o'clock when quiet hours began the last of them sputtered into silence. The tent campers all stood up and applauded. The wild returned and hovered close, opening our senses like night-blooming flowers. We glimpsed the world our ancestors knew, mysterious and vast. That edge of fear, exhilaration. The hidden waterfall plunged in the darkness. Somewhere in the distance a coyote found its voice.

At Narrow Gauge, I opened my eyes and picked up my pen and lay line after line over the page as the memories kept coming, all of them having to do with noise or places where I used to get away.

When I was growing up, trips to the mountains taught me a quiet that I measured by my ability to stand on a ridge and hear the small white sound of a river in the valley far below. A raven's hoarse report, swallowed by a vast and intimidating silence, a silence that thrilled me. At home near Sea-Tac airport, I sprawled on the lawn with a book and jammed my fingers into my ears every few minutes as a jet shrieked overhead. The airport grew and the jets grew louder and the country roads swelled into busy thoroughfares. By the time I was in high school I was antsy for escape.

Few of my neighbors seemed to miss the vanishing quiet as they howled at the inanities of *Laugh-In*, hacked gas-powered mowers through the dirt clods in their lawns, and adjusted without comment to the constant drone that drifted from the newly built section of Interstate 5 a few miles away. No one seemed to wonder where the quiet had gone, and true to its nature, it slipped away unnoticed.

On a trip home to Washington with my husband years later, we stopped at a state park on the east slope of the Cascades where my family used to camp. The lake I remembered was tucked into a lacy forest of ponderosa pine, where people pitched vast Army surplus canvas tents and rowed across the lake to fish the deep water under a cliff of solemn gray. The lake smelled of trees and sunlight, sweet as a rich dessert, a place where we collected pinecones and wandered barefoot on mats of fallen needles. The only sounds were squirrels scolding, water lapping at the lakeshore, the hollow bang of an oar against a wooden gunwale in the blue dusk.

"It's a beautiful spot," I promised Don. "You'll love it."

When we arrived the parking lot overflowed with RVs the size of busses and pickup trucks hauling boats of every size and shape. Car stereos blared. The water churned with the crossing wakes of Sea Squirrels, Jet-skis, and what looked to me like miniature hydroplanes. A fisherman of my father's generation would have been left rocking in his rowboat, bewildered. Pickups without mufflers turned tight loops in the parking lot, mimicking the paths of the boats on the water below. Noise echoed through the trees and washed against the gray cliff on the far side of the lake.

I looked for something recognizable—a pinecone on the ground, a footpath leading into shadows. Perhaps I had the wrong lake. Could this be the place where my father once stood, cleaning trout in his red plaid swimming trunks while my mother sat at the picnic table and painted her toenails frost pink?

I turned to Don. "Let's get out of here."

"It's too bad," he said. Trying to be helpful, he added, "The lake I used to go in the Adirondacks is the same way."

I didn't consider myself an ultra-sensitive aesthete, disturbed by every sound. I could see the way others jumped at a sudden horn blare or barking dog, the way they paused in conversation on a street corner as a noisy vehicle went by. In the city people went indoors to escape noise, where they missed any chance of hearing natural sounds. As public outdoor spaces became increasingly crowded and noisy, only the wealthy could buy enough space to surround themselves with outdoor quiet. In America, the land of equal rights, this condition felt wrong.

My pen stopped moving and I laid aside my notebook. Perhaps it was time to close my eyes again, for instead of enjoying the afternoon of quiet

I was getting myself worked up, recalling angry letters to the *Jackson Hole News* about airport noise and replaying every harsh and unwelcome sound I could remember. I might as well have been a teenager, reading with her fingers in her ears.

Minutes passed, and I heard only the musical tones of water drops splashing on travertine. The breeze died, the nuthatch flitted away. Before I knew it, the airplanes and motorboats had retreated as well and there was no memory of noise, no expectation of noise to come, only the present moment, infused by the quiet at Narrow Gauge. A rare stillness of mind ventured forward, like a doe stepping into the open to shake after a summer rain.

"Let's share a little of what we did today," Deborah suggested when we reassembled. "There's no hurry to go."

We sat in a sleepy circle and passed around sketchbooks and objects we had found—bits of fruit-rind agate and transparent travertine, a silica and lime-encrusted pinecone.

Deborah shared a few lines that would later coalesce into a poem:

> I am the wind
> Sweeping the surface of a pool,
> I am the ribbon of steam
> Gusting skyward,
> I am the lazy tendril
> Drifting down a scalloped terrace.

Cinda recalled her adolescence in a voice barely above a whisper. "Wildness," she read. "A woman gone mad. Once I thought myself daring, now I call it stupid. The bliss was extraordinary, beyond what I feel now."

We leaned forward and held our breaths, waiting for what she would say next. Her eyes shone as she looked up from her notebook.

"I felt it again," she said. "The wildness, after this, today."

My turn. I flipped through the pages in my notebook and glanced over the lame and clumsy words, most of them crossed out. "I don't have anything to read," I said. "I spent the whole time thinking about airplanes and motorboats and worrying that pretty soon there will be no place left to find any quiet."

"Same here," someone else said.

"Me too."

"What can we do?"

People sat thoughtfully, echoing each other, nodding in agreement, and Deborah grabbed the reins.

"Well then, what shall we do? This is a truth we need to put out there, how should we go about it? What can each of us do to help preserve the quiet?"

We slowly went around the circle, offering ideas. A letter to the Park Service, another to the editorial page. One to the manufacturers of diesel pickups. Whatever was offered was given in a gentle voice, each spoken word blending into song. John's baritone, Cinda's whisper, reedy as a flute. The words and voices repeated a blessing, the gift of quiet we would carry with us when we left.

Quiet, by its nature, slips away unnoticed. But once it's gone, we notice. In Yellowstone, a long-standing controversy over snowmobiles is largely about noise. The debate surrounding scenic overflights in the Grand Canyon is all about noise. Noise, or the more recent bureaucratic substitute, "excessive sound," only makes the list of threats to the National Parks when decibels begin to cause physical damage to eardrums. Compared to ecological calamities such as the replacement of native plants by alien weeds, the pollution of pristine lakes, and the brown haze that hovers over many national parks and forests, noise is considered a lesser evil—a matter of aesthetics.

We shouldn't have to make this kind of choice. We are fond of saying the national parks are sacred, but we don't always act as if we believe it. Our relationship with these public wild lands has become abstract, intermittent, and removed from our daily concerns—while the priceless refuge they offer from the distractions of our lives is increasingly at risk. We appreciate the wild through coffee table books and National Geographic specials on PBS, or we sign up for packaged vacations guaranteed to deliver "memorable outdoor experiences"—followed by a five-star hotel room and chilled chardonnay. We've grown to accept, or even expect, a theme park rather than the wild.

Without authentic and individual experience, without the practiced intimacy needed to grow a personal relationship with real places, we cannot muster the visceral allegiance to them that is so urgently needed. I worry that the lack of intimate knowledge of the outdoors and its attendant quiet will make us simply forget about both. Silence will go the way of the Dodo, unnoticed and unmourned.

Soda Butte Creek, Yellowstone National Park.

Quiet, the precious commodity of our time. At Narrow Gauge, our little group resolved to search for it, defend it, and never let it slip away unnoticed.

On the last day of the workshop, Deborah herded us into the van to another of her secret unknown spots. She called this place The Promontory. We fanned out for individual writing time, and I sought shelter from the hot summer wind in the lee of a granite boulder, a glacial erratic that must have traveled on its conveyor belt of ice all the way from the Beartooth Mountains. The Yellowstone River ran below. Downstream, the water disappeared among the cliffs of a tall, bare-faced mountain.

Hellroaring Mountain. With its conical form and stony gray face lined by long spiral cracks, it resembled a hornet nest. Straddling the park boundary, it stood like a guard at the southern boundary of the Absaroka-Beartooth Wilderness. *My wilderness.* The words came to mind unexpectedly and with startling ferocity. I stared across the Yellowstone River and Hellroaring Mountain stared back, making me remember.

After six years in Wyoming, I was surprised that my difficult years in Montana returned with such force. I had not expected to crest a ridge in Yellowstone and be stopped in my tracks by the sight of a mountain, flooded by memories I had tucked safely out of sight. I sat down with my back against the boulder and remembered, writing all that came to mind

Glacial erratics near The Promontory, Yellowstone National Park.

in my notebook. Perhaps it was the act of writing that helped purge my bitterness, for when I looked up from the page Hellroaring Mountain had lost its ominous appearance, now as neutral and benign as any other point along the ridge. It was the Yellowstone River that bound me to the place where I now lived and to the places I had been, from the headwaters in the Teton Wilderness to the tributaries downstream originating deep within the Gallatin National Forest. I could venture downstream to remember and forgive, and if necessary I could retreat upstream to where I felt more comfortable. It was all the same river, reaching into the heart of the same mountain wilderness, the place that I called home.

We gathered around a campfire the final evening of the course. When my turn came to read, I finally had something to say. I read every page of what I had written that afternoon at The Promontory, including memories of having been part of the "crack crew" and other indignities I had suffered. It felt good to read without inhibition, knowing that my audience was kind and supportive. When I finished, one woman came up to me with tears in her eyes.

"You have to tell this story," she said.

I hugged her. "Thanks," I said. "I think I just did."

18

THE YEARS FOLLOWING MY FLASH OF INSIGHT about home and place at The Promontory were times of change in the Forest Service, although not all of the changes pointed the agency in a single direction. Jack Ward Thomas, a respected wildlife professional who had spent his career with the Forest Service, was appointed chief in 1994, and those of us who saw our mission as one of conservation were encouraged. He spoke of ecosystems, science-based decision making, and reverence for the priceless resource we were employed to care for.

Then came the Gingrich-led Congress of 1995. One of the first things this Congress did was to change the name of the long-standing Natural Resource Committee to simply "Resource Committee." Even the word natural was too green for this crew, and that small word change set the tone for a time when the national forests directly felt the effects of what was going on in Washington. During the holidays in 1995–96, when Congress and the President could not agree on the budget, we were furloughed for three weeks while the government essentially shut down. With the South Entrance to Yellowstone closed, snowmobile outfitters with clients booked for Christmas turned to the national forest. A guest ranch twenty-five miles up the Greys River that served lunches in the winter had a capacity of about twenty people in its dining room; for three weeks it served more than two hundred per day.

In addition to a swing away from Chief Thomas's ecosystem-friendly vision, the Forest Service was faced with a series of budget cuts. Each year brought a few hundred thousand dollars less to the Bridger-Teton's recreation, trails, and wilderness programs. At the same time, recreation use in the national forests surrounding Yellowstone was booming. Gone was the quiet time between Labor Day and Memorial Day, as more people took to the woods on mountain bikes, ATVs, snowshoes, and snowmobiles.

The traditional days-long backpack and horse pack trips that had once been a mainstay gave way to vacations in which people wanted to do a little of everything. Keeping up with the burgeoning human uses and their effects on forest wild land, while budgets continued to decline, required a tremendous amount of innovation on the part of district-level recreation managers. Some were not up to the task, and the condition of campgrounds and trails deteriorated.

In the late 1990s another Forest Service chief, this one recruited from the BLM, listed four primary threats to national forest system lands: fuel build-up, which created the potential for catastrophic wildfires; invasive species (weeds, aquatic invertebrates, non-native wildlife); loss of open space due to rapid development of forest land; and unmanaged recreation—by which was meant use of motor vehicles away from designated roads and trails. When the individual forests requested funding for projects from trail bridges to visitor center displays, it was required that we explain how each request would help alleviate one or more of the four threats.

From my position, working at a forest that was still largely wild and threat-free, the main thing we needed was a sustained level of funding from year to year, so trained and skilled field crews could do the job of maintaining what we already had: fifty campgrounds, three thousand miles of trail, uncountable trailheads, boat launches, and waysides with tables and toilets to clean. This work fell into the "operation and maintenance" category, for which there was no specific funding above the base level, and for which we depended largely on the seasonal workforce—temporary employees who did not receive benefits and had no guarantee of employment from year to year. Beyond the base-level funds distributed to the forests annually, which barely covered permanent salaries, the forests competed for pots of money reserved for special purposes.

At the same time, a national effort to reduce staff and increase private contracting began. We were asked to conduct study after study, comparing the relative efficiency of work done by Forest Service employees to that done by contractors. Consolidation of administrative functions such as personnel hiring and purchasing spawned an array of new computer-based systems and required a week of phone tag with someone in Albuquerque instead of a quick trip down the hallway to ask the budget analyst a question. Employees who had specialized in the maintenance and repair of computers were herded into information-technology service

Musk thistle, an invasive weed, on state land adjacent to the Bridger-Teton National Forest.

centers or given other jobs to do, and were not allowed to use their skills to help staff like me. Instead, we placed a call to the End User Support Center (whose acronym EUSC was pronounced 'you suck'), where we spent the first fifteen minutes of our call explaining to the technician who we were and where we worked.

I believed, as did many colleagues, that the changes were intended to waste our time and make us less efficient, thus making the case for farming out more of the work to private contractors. Whether intentional or not, decreased efficiency was certainly the result.

The effort to privatize the Forest Service extended to the forests themselves. Elected officials in the West had long campaigned to turn federal land holdings over to the states, which would in turn sell valuable parcels with potential for padding the states' sagging budgets. The BLM had been their primary target for years, but national forest lands were being eyed with new interest as land values in places like Teton County, Wyoming, continued their steep climb from the late 1980s.

This was the backdrop in which I and others attempted to continue working on the parts of our jobs we considered the most essential—caring for the land and serving people, in agency parlance. Retirement was still years away, but I started thinking about it with longing. As a birthday

Ruts made by illegal 4WD travel, Bridger-Teton National Forest.

gift one year, I received these items from fellow employees: a battery-operated tranquility fountain that brought the soft sound of trickling water to my office, a bottle of herbs and flower petals whose scent promised calm, and a coffee cup with an altered Forest Service shield emblazoned on it, reading "Forest Circus—Department of Aggravation."

In the late 1990s, having worked for the Forest Service for close to twenty years, I began to wake to a recurring dream, in which I plodded through heavy knee-deep snow, away from a small white house. I understood that I had left the house for some purpose, but as I paused, afraid to continue, I couldn't remember if I was hurrying to catch something unseen beyond my dream or trying to escape the little house. Panic tugged at my sleeve and I hesitated, aware of the snow becoming denser and more resistant to my effort. I struggled to pull each foot along as though walking against a current, and soon found that my legs could no longer move at all. Panic nudged me awake.

After one of these dreams, alert in the dark stillness of my bedroom in the middle of the night, I had this revelation: the dream was about my job.

It was April, and winter was beginning to soften into spring. The birds returned, species by species: American robin, red-winged blackbird, mountain bluebird, Canada goose. Aspens poised to bloom, with silver globes ready to drop into long rose-gray tassels at the first hint of warm air. After brittle frosts every night, bursts of rain began to replace the snow squalls.

The meaning of my dream waited at the boundary of my conscious mind while a notebook lay open in my lap to receive a line or two between long periods of watching out the upstairs window. The dream-snow's heaviness remained in my legs while I turned the pages of a notebook to a list I had made the year before, of what I called values and principles—the litany I used in an attempt to keep myself focused on what mattered most, rather than becoming distracted by the many crises at work that were urgent but not very important. Distractions had been coming my way more frequently in recent years, as the Forest Service entered the throes of fundamental change in the way it conducted business. My purpose was the careful and reverent stewardship of public lands, not feeding a database or attending mandatory training on computer security.

That list served as an antidote for a restlessness that had been growing for some time. My profession, to which I had dedicated most of my adult life, did not satisfy me anymore. I had helped write forest plans and provided text and illustrations for countless brochures and newsletters. I had overseen the management of campgrounds, trails, and backcountry. Government jargon labeled me a "staff officer," one of those quasi-military titles meant to convey power and authority. Or so I believed when I was in college and working summer jobs at the local ranger district. A visit from one of the professional staff officers from the supervisor's office was a momentous event indeed. To have him actually talk to me felt as though I had been granted a special favor.

I collected degrees in subjects I thought would get me outdoor work, to reach the heights belonging to those staff officers. Forests lay like mist on my mind as I stepped from the actual mist of early morning through the familiar double doors of Haggart Hall. I walked into a cave of bare concrete with moss-green walls the color of rocks beside a waterfall, past corkboards fluttering with announcements and the giant terrarium where Casey the bull snake lived, and into Lecture Room 125 for winter quarter chemistry. This was a serious class, not one of those "basket weaving" classes that one took to pad a grade point average. My load each term was full of meaty courses and labs, most of them held in the basement of that science building. When I left my last lab at five o'clock I once again stepped through the double doors, into the gray of dusk.

Now I wished that I had taken basket weaving, had run my hands through the dried lengths of smooth reed grass and knobby willow wands and splints of vegetable-dyed ash. Weaving strands of native fiber into useful and beautiful objects would have brought me closer to the forest than biology classes ever did.

My old career goal, long achieved, was beginning to lose its luster. For too many years I allowed the job to eat at me, waking up in the middle of the night to worry about things I could not influence. I had long grown impatient with bureaucratic inertia and a conformity that made anyone who questioned it a target.

A flutter of wings caught my attention as pine siskins chased each other through the blooming aspen, chirping brightly as they swelled with the yellow wing coverts of breeding plumage. Sunlight pierced the margin of a cloud and the season rose up like a flower ready to burst into bloom. How could I feel restless, even bored, in the face of these wonders? Even as I chastised myself, I saw my restlessness as necessary to later understanding. What once brought me comfort and security had begun to imprison me. Only when imprisonment displaced security would I be ready for change.

But what would I change? If the job I had once dreamt of in a place I loved was not good enough, what was? I didn't want a job but a vocation, and for much of my career I thought I had one. But the combination of age, a shift in the kind of work I was being asked to do, and a stifling sense of having seen it all before made me wonder if I had been imagining my life as I wished it to be instead of living it as it was. I found myself, as I opened my office e-mail and prepared for another budget meeting, yearning for creative, life-affirming work.

Creativity lived, not at the office, but in flowerbeds and studios and kitchens, among growing, graceful, and delicious things. It thrived in the hills as they brightened from straw-brown to lime-green, and out my window where I watched the siskins gracing the aspen branches.

Sometimes I felt guilty for taking a day off work to watch birds, especially in the spring when the earth itself seemed to take a long, satisfied inhalation. I told myself that when I died I would not look back and wish

Planning the day's route with staff officer Gloria Flora and Pinedale District wilderness manager Betsy Ballard, Bridger Wilderness, 1990.

I had spent more time at the office. Play was the real work of our lives, *re-creation*.

Out the window, the aspen tree bent against an approaching squall. I allowed the notebook to fall closed in my lap, still puzzling over the oldest question of all: who am I? Who, of all people, should know better the answer to this question? Yet, I could not answer it that day, unable to see myself without a professional disguise. Like the emperor's new clothes, the job in which I cloaked myself might have been more transparent to others than it was to me.

Who was anyone besides a name, a job, a place in the community? Attributes by which we identified and recognized each other. The details of one's surface appearance brought the person into focus and made her familiar. But did they tell me who she was? I had long defined myself by details of what I did and thought, but they failed to tell me who I am.

My friends at work did not seem to ponder such questions. They bustled with activity, planning parties and tending to the affairs of their children. They seemed content and self-possessed, while I wandered the halls and glanced around my office feeling lost. I searched for some deeper, undiscovered part of myself, a part that cried to be recognized beneath the order and routine of daily living. Did my life have some meaning beyond what I gave it? I was told as a child that God had some kind of grand plan for me, and all I needed was faith to learn its nature. Perhaps the grand plan for each of us was to find our own true path, by ourselves.

I worried that, in my effort to reveal the true nature of the self, I would find a person far different from the one I thought I knew. An entity who waited for my discovery and who couldn't care less what I did to earn a living. The realization frightened me, since rewards had always come to me for things I had achieved. I feared that beneath the emperor's clothes lay a daydreamer watching the birds; an idler staring out the window at slanting rain and aspen trees. It worried me more to know that I found something wrong with that.

My identity, clothed as a professional, was the small white house of my dream, safe and predictable, lit against the unknown snowy night. I stepped off the porch and tried to run across the yard, into the dark and silent forest. But I was too afraid and my legs would not propel me any longer, so I turned back toward the light, wondering what had prompted me to leave. The hold of the familiar threatened to keep me from discovering the possible.

If I was bored with anything, it was with what I saw as necessary striving, achieving, and guarding my self-image. A boredom so incongruous with the time of year when all the world was quickening, it made me realize how far from my true self I had wandered. A pulse ran through the thawing earth and up the aspen trees, a message whispered ground to branch, picked up by the feet of birds and spread across the sky on their wing beats. Spring was the pulse I wanted to place my hand on, to hold my ear to the ground and listen for, a rhythm inviting me to dance. Spring bloomed, while I dreamt about lamp-lit houses on snowy nights.

Perhaps I was acting out my own vernal ritual, like a new leaf pushing off the leathery scale that protected it all winter. I had outgrown a husk that sheltered me long and well, that gave me something to call myself and a place in the everyday world. I was not yet ready to let it go, not ready to brave the uncertainty that waited. But when I felt the husk I longed to shed, I knew it was too small to contain me.

I needed a job and mine was a good one. Yet I wondered if I was used up, expendable, in need of replacement. Papers stacked up in the in-box that I labeled *Do Soon*. Every day more of them arrived, and the *Do Soon* box became a stagnant eddy. I culled it every few weeks and found nothing so urgent after all. What if they replaced me with someone younger and more energetic? She would keep the in-box clean. Let her, I thought. Adding to the concerns swirling in my head were thoughts about my father. He had not written in several months, and he was on my mind when I called my mother a few days before.

"Your Dad has a tumor in his lungs," she told me.

"How long has it been there?" I asked.

"How should I know, he doesn't tell me anything."

"What's he going to do about it?"

"Why don't you ask him."

"I've been meaning to write to him anyway," I said.

"Fine." She changed the subject to her cat.

After talking to my mother I called Dad. "Do you want me to come?" I asked.

"No, no. The doctors don't know for sure yet," he said.

Dad was uncomfortable as ever on the telephone, so I hung up quickly and told him I would write. Now I pondered the letter, setting aside my notebook and taking up a blank sheet of paper. What I wanted to tell him and what he would most want to hear were not necessarily the same. References to affection would cause great embarrassment, I knew, but

The author with pack llama "B Flat" heading into the wilderness.

I also thought that anyone who was seventy-eight and had just gotten the news that he might have lung cancer would appreciate hearing that someone loved him. I thought about how it would feel when he was gone, now that we finally had a relationship, one in which we shared more of our deepest selves, experiences, and opinions than I thought possible. But I couldn't use phrases such as when you're gone, or I will miss you— because the doctors didn't know for sure, after all. This was another approaching change in my life over which I had no control and to which I must adjust.

That year, I was often drawn into shops around town that I had rarely visited, the ones that sold incense and perfume. I bought a bottle of bright purple ink for my fountain pen. I imagined wearing clothes of soft, flowing gauze that draped loosely from my shoulders. My closet bulged with somber gray flannel and navy-blue, colors that suggested professional respectability. But, I thought with delight, when I started wearing gauze, I would follow the fragrance of perfume wafting out of shop doors. I would relish the balance of the pen in my hand as its nib doodled in purple ink.

My office was an intolerable mess with its loosely rolled maps and stacks of paper and three-ring binders perching on the tops of bookcases. One day while everyone else was traveling with their families during Jackson Hole's two-week spring break, I pulled up a chair and a wastebasket and set to work. Copies of memos I wrote, staff papers I labored over, proposals that never bore fruit. A budget report that once seemed imperative. (I cancelled a wilderness pack trip to finish it on time, only to learn that I was the only staffer who had turned it in by the due date, so the date was set back two weeks.) The pages dropped like falling leaves into the trash.

I envied young mothers and retirees who stayed at home and puttered in their gardens on weekday mornings in the spring. Yet I was afraid, once again. If I were in their places, I would wish to be back in the buzzing, humming thick of things, productive and needed and busy. Slowly it was dawning on me that there is no thick-of-things. I had created a whirlwind of activity and I spun around in it until I was tired and dizzy and ready to leap off.

No wonder I felt disoriented: I was in the middle of a leap.

The author's desk, Bridger-Teton National Forest supervisor's office.

One day I found myself staring for over a minute at my reflection in the bathroom mirror. Most mornings I glanced toward the glass to watch my toothbrush stirring up a pale mint foam but paid no attention to who was glancing back. Now I leaned against the sink as if looking into the eyes of a fascinating stranger. I realized I hardly knew the person gazing back.

Familiar only with the reflection that brushed her teeth while tugging at an earring, multi-tasking before running downstairs and out the door, I stared at this new person who watched me as the clock ticked, unnoticed. She looked strangely serene, calm as a statue. I could see that she was a follower of songbirds, an idler in the aspens, a woman who owed much to her long-estranged and rediscovered father. She wore a kind and patient expression as she waited for me to introduce myself.

I thought of her as I sat watching out the window at the bright April day. When would she visit again? The siskins dispersed and I had despaired of finding the right words to send my father. Then I caught a tiny movement near my face. A spider hung from the ceiling on a filament of silk, her legs tucked so tightly she resembled a speck of dust or a minute flake of tree bark. All at once she dropped another foot. I caught the strand of silk and lowered her to the floor.

19

A PEARL-BLUE OVERCAST HOVERED in the mountains, an omen of impending snow. I walked along the trail in Cache Creek, knowing that the next day I might find dry ground again, or a foot of fresh November powder that would put an end to the hiking season. The wind stiffened under buckling clouds and I quickened my pace.

My destination was a stand of aspens whose trunks stood straight as flagpoles for twenty feet, and whose crowns kinked and corkscrewed and pretzel-twisted as if grafted onto the wrong stems. This little clone had offered company and contemplative quiet when I was lost and confused, my shortcomings many and my small achievements profoundly disappointing. It brought comfort when the events far beyond the insular world of Jackson Hole became hard for me to bear.

I hiked for a couple of miles before leaving the trail to walk uphill through clumps of cured grass and dried wildflower stalks, over fallen logs, and through brambles of snowberry and wild rose. Entering the aspen stand that I called the "twisty trunks" felt like walking into a nave, with asymmetrical but graceful arches overhead. A sapling lodgepole pine in the understory marked the spot I chose to sit or lie back in the dry grass. In the years since I started going there the pine turned brown and died but remained standing, as if holding the seat for my arrival.

I found my seat on the floor of the aspen nave and absorbed what surrounded me: the crunch of brome grass under my legs, the season's last flies and spiders hurrying to their unknown destinations, the rattle of the rising wind in bare branches. To the west, the frontal hills of the Gros Ventre Range opened like a pair of wings, forested Snow King Mountain on one side and the sage- and aspen-covered hills opposite. Rendezvous Peak and Mt. Glory stood across the valley in the distance.

The twisty trees, a few miles from my house, reminded me that beauty was not confined to the farthest ridges. They reveled in the November wind just as they did under a high spring sun. Each season brought a singular joyful music to the aspens: the rustling of summer leaves, the clatter of bare branches, the hum of the spring's first wild bees visiting the catkins. Among them I lay on my back and rubbed my shoulders into the smoky musk of fallen leaves, nearly burrowing underground to join the clone of aspens at its core.

Among the twisty trees I filled my pail with sweet cold water from the well of wonder, fortification for the quest for understanding, the search for consequence in my brief passage in this world. Brief passages were heavy on my mind: my father had died in early June at the age of eighty-three. Two months ago, four planes hijacked by terrorists had ended the lives of thousands. A sense of bewilderment still infused every conversation, and every evening the television news began with updates on progress at what the New York Port Authority had come to call The Pile. The pile was still smoking two months on. We continued with our lives, our work, with an increased desire to give them meaning.

My heart was sore from the events of September 11, and empty from the loss of my father. The twisty-trunked aspens brought comfort, for

Aspen stand with twisty trunks, Bridger-Teton National Forest.

they welcomed me into their wild congregation. I found communion with the leaves, now fallen and gone gray, whose brief lives were spent collecting blemishes, insect tunnels, and scars before they settled to the earth to feed the soil. In life and death, the leaves remained an essential part of something more, every phase from spring bud to November leaf-mold infused with purpose.

On Memorial Day, 2001, I had walked into my father's room at Seatoma Convalescent Center south of Seattle. He was propped up on a pillow reading, and when he saw me, he said, "Susan!" I took his hands and kissed his forehead, for he was too frail to hug. His limbs reminded me of dowel rods, no muscle tone remaining. His teeth were rotten, his toenails long, thick, and yellow. But his eyes shone and he smiled with genuine delight.

I stayed for four days, visiting for an hour at a time while Don took our Labrador for walks. I read, brought him leaves from trees that he had loved, and sat beside his bed while he slept. Brief visits to my mother in her condo a few miles away were enough to satisfy her. At eighty-two, she appeared to be taking care of herself, dusting less frequently than I remembered, but her living space was orderly and the condo was well laid out. When I visited her I was glad to have the dog as a subject of conversation. She allowed him into her condo and palavered over him, much to the disgust of her cat. She told me she had not visited my father and didn't intend to.

"I'm sorry you feel that way," I said.

She ignored me and continued to address my dog with baby talk.

Each time I saw my father he had grown weaker. We spent less time in conversation and he slept more. The last time I saw him I kissed his forehead before leaving the room. "I'm going to miss you," I said. He had already dozed off.

Months after my father fell ill, he was still telling me that the doctors were not sure. He said not to worry; he felt fine. At the end of his life, he had been grateful, satisfied with all he had achieved and the choices he had made. I envied him his acceptance of whatever came, with apparently little concern. It was a privilege to be with him as he faded from lucidity into the endless sleep.

The day we left Seattle, I made a final visit to my mother. I went alone while Don walked the dog, and she spent the twenty minutes asking me how the dog was. I insisted on telling her how my father was. If she didn't take the chance to visit now, it would soon be too late. When I left, she stood on the small balcony of her second-floor condo and told me that she loved me. I didn't know it then, but that was the last visit I had with her during which we had an exchange that resembled conversation. I found closure with both of my parents that week.

My mother had become adept at hiding her increasing dementia when I talked to her on the telephone, and I was good at failing to see it. She searched for words, asked the same questions several times, and told the same stories. But she had been doing this for years, especially when she had too much gin in her, so she didn't sound very different to me.

She refused to soften her attitude toward my father, even when he lay helpless in a hospital bed filling his diaper with uncontrolled diarrhea. But her hardened heart did nothing to dissolve the decades during which they had been tied to one another, and after he died she declined more rapidly. In the early spring of 2003 a nurse at Valley Medical Center called to inform me that my mother had been admitted with severe dehydration and multiple bruises. She had apparently fallen in her condo bathroom, perhaps after having a stroke, and had lain on the floor in there for two days before her neighbors got worried and called the police. They broke down the door and found her.

When I saw her at the hospital, she looked as if she had been beaten, her thin skin blooming with purple blotches. She said she was glad to see me, but I noticed she said that to all the nurses and aides who helped her. When she was strong enough to leave the hospital, she went into the same nursing home where she wouldn't visit my father. I spent most of the week taking care of legal and financial arrangements. She had always been meticulous about her finances, her checkbook kept up-to-date and balanced in her neat, small handwriting. But I discovered that she hadn't filed income tax reports for the past four years, and her checkbook was a mess of scrawl and crossings-out. Until she fell, she continued to convince me that her mental state, while short on memory, was not as bad as it must have been. After her fall, the decline was precipitous.

When I visited the nursing home, it was clear she had no idea who I was, other than a nice lady who came to see her, hold her hand, and feed her chocolates. I showed her photographs of her condo and she didn't recognize the place. A picture of her beloved cat brought no reaction either. "I'd like to have a cat someday," she said.

Left: Hugh Paul Marsh, age eighty-two; *right:* Virginia Marsh, age eighty-two.

Friends had told me how upsetting it had been when their demented parents no longer knew them, but for me it was a relief. It didn't matter that she forgot who I was, for she had also forgotten her lifelong resentments and anger. It was as if she had begun her mental life again, as a two-year-old with a poor grasp of language, but with great satisfaction over small pleasures like a piece of candy.

She passed away in 2006, at the age of eighty-seven. I had her ashes sent to Wyoming, and set the box next to the one containing my father's remains. "Try to get along, you two," I told them. My mother's ashes are now buried at her family farm in Ohio. Dad remains with me, until I have a chance to take them to the Duwamish Waterway, near the Ballard Locks, where we went to watch a few small salmon climb the concrete ladder.

The author doing what she does best, cleaning up an abandoned campsite in the backcountry, 1991.

20

DON'S SISTER HARRIET, whose Forest Service career inspired my decision to pursue one myself, retired in 1999. The last five years will go quickly, she promised, and though I doubted it at the time, they did. I had never forgotten the first conversation I had with Joe when I moved to Montana. He retired on his fifty-fifth birthday, the first hour he was eligible, and I promised myself then that I would do the same.

My last few years with the Forest Service held some frustrations—three years of concentrated work on forest plan revision, a revision that was dropped when the forest planner transferred to another job and the position remained vacant. But they included accomplishments I will always remember with fondness: citizen-based management plans for three wildernesses; two summers of field assessments of developed campgrounds forest-wide with the timber staff officer, as we prepared vegetation management plans for each site; passage of the Craig Thomas Legacy Act for the Wyoming Range and Snake River Headwaters. By 2009 I was finishing work on a hiking and natural history guide and looking forward to having more time to write. In March of that year the legacy acts were signed into law, and I began work on comprehensive river management plans for the three hundred miles of newly designated Wild and Scenic Rivers within the forest. Some of my favorite streams were included in the Act, thanks to the inventory I led after settling a forest plan appeal years before.

Yet, on a daily basis, my work had become more stressful due to unplanned and urgent requests that I could only respond to by putting off a project with its own due date. Younger people were joining the organization, and I was ready to step aside and let them take over. The sense of propriety I once had in relation to a national forest was slipping away and I looked forward to enjoying the places I loved as a citizen without feeling responsible for every weed or wad of toilet paper I found along the trail.

Left: Harriet Plumley, retired USFS researcher and planner; *right:* the author's retirement party, February 2010.

In September I announced my retirement for the following February. My boss, Pam, began talking about a mega-party involving a weekend of skiing and hot-tubbing, an idea which, to my surprise, I savored. After years of being slighted, insulted, and left out, I had at last found acceptance, and I looked forward to ending my thirty years with the Forest Service on a high note. Between drafting chapters for the river management plans, I cleaned my office, sorting and discarding the leavings of a career. I found that I was clearing out my mind as well, ready to start again.

My retirement party sparkled with elegance, thanks to the generosity of Pam, who had used most of a recent cash award to help pay for it. "They gave me the award for a project you led," she said. "So it seemed like the right thing to do." Over half of those attending were friends from out of town or non-agency pals from various conservation and writing groups. It reminded me of the potlucks I once held at my house in Montana, and I used the occasion to give thanks to those I worked with and who helped transform my once-rocky career into a pleasure. I looked back on what I had influenced, from restoring old campsites to the wild to leading wilderness and other special-area plans that used public participation in innovative ways. Specialist input on all kinds of projects; the friendships I treasured. Somehow the wounds had healed over time and I found much to celebrate.

What lay before me now was the remainder of life, and my choices for contributing in new ways to conservation of precious public land. I

Left: Joe Gutkowski, age eighty-three, hunting elk in the Gallatin National Forest; *right:* Wag in his seventies, at his home in Leadore, Idaho.

considered those I called mentors: Bill Worf, Marsha Kearney, Rich Inman, Gloria Flora, Tom Kovalicky, Bob Glenn, Alma Winward, Ross McPherson, and of course my pal Joe Gutkowski. What had these people done since leaving the Forest Service? In order, this: founder of the organization Wilderness Watch; small business owner and philanthropist; horsepacker and ice fisherman extraordinaire; founder of Sustainable Obtainable Solutions and star of the lecture circuit; professional fly fishing guide; red-rock canyoneer; consulting plant ecologist; farmer and landscaper; and environmental crusader (if there was a "save the snails" group, Joe's wife Millie told me, he would join.). These people, and many others, supported and inspired me. All of them conducted themselves honorably as public servants before seeking their new paths. I vowed to follow in their footsteps.

Between the summer of 1974, when I took my first seasonal job, and my retirement in 2010, the Forest Service made impressive progress in the arena of cultural diversity. Women now accounted for close to 40 percent of the agency's workforce, though the preponderance of the jobs they held fell into the clerical and administrative categories. When I started as a permanent employee in 1980, professional women served as junior foresters, research scientists, and mid-level resource specialists. None were being "groomed" for line positions. By the time I retired, the agency had appointed one female chief, several associate and deputy chiefs, a regional forester or two, and many forest supervisors and district rangers. To quote a March 2012 online article from the Forest Service office of communications:

> Given today's opportunities offered to employees of the Forest Service, regardless of gender, race and other backgrounds, it's difficult to imagine the agency as it was over a century ago.
>
> Veteran firefighter and acting Associate Deputy Chief of the National Forest System Patti Hirami is still having fun, even 20 years after she joined the Forest Service.
>
> "I've had tremendous opportunities with the agency," Hirami said. "The opportunities to do almost anything you want are here with the Forest Service."

I imagined how encouraging this would sound to anyone interested in the status of women in the workplace. Until I read the single comment that had been posted below the article, which said this:

> I'm a new USDA Forest Service employee and would love to continue my career; however, I've been subjected to the below:
>
> - Sexual jokes
> - Attempted assaults
> - Reprisal for reporting malfeasances
> - Slanderous and libel statements
> - Stalking
> - Intimidation
> - Mismanagement
> - Fraud, Waste, and Abuse and threats to not report same
> - Witnessed employees spend hours daily on government computers chatting on Facebook and Yahoo
> - Threats to end my career for having spoken the truth

Together, those blog posts tell the story of the Forest Service—it has changed greatly, and mostly for the better. And some things will never change.

Alma Winward and wildlife habitat monitoring crew measuring willow growth, Bridger-Teton National Forest.

While the advancement of women within the Forest Service during the past few decades is a statistical fact, statistics don't offer much insight about how well each woman has handled herself. Some that I have known were excellent, honest, and brave. Some were pushed into positions that did not suit them, while others actively sought those positions, and not entirely for the right reasons. I have worked for female managers who treated employees as if they were personal servants, and who seemed to have forgotten who their real bosses were (citizens) and who paid their salaries (citizens, again). This attitude was, of course, not limited to women.

Though gender politics have followed me and my colleagues for our entire careers, I look forward to a day when gender no longer matters. It matters far less than personal integrity, and the Forest Service needs leaders who rely on sound science and high quality staff work, who can hear and absorb many competing arguments, and are willing to make decisions based on informed judgments. The agency's reward system does not encourage such leadership. It encourages forest supervisors to tell the regional foresters what they want to hear so they, in turn, can relay the happy talk on to the chief's office. In the final week before the 1995–96 government shutdown, I sat in on a conference call among the Intermountain Region's forest supervisors and RO staff. Each forest took its turn reporting how their employees were coping with the imminent Christmastime furlough. One after another raised his voice to a mock-cheerful pitch and claimed that everything and everyone was just fine. When the Bridger-Teton had its turn (we had gone in reverse-alphabetical order, starting with the Wasatch) our supervisor was quiet for a moment, then she said, "People are really worried. There's a high stress level, especially with our lower grade employees who are counting on that paycheck."

The silence that followed lasted long enough to become uncomfortable and someone in the RO quickly stepped in to change the subject.

Like the military, NASA, and dozens of other government agencies, the Forest Service is a top-down bureaucracy. The drive for consistency in the application of laws and regulations notwithstanding, specific management decisions for a particular place must be done at the local level in collaboration with the public. Only the savviest can negotiate the pull of these opposites, a dichotomy that has dogged the Forest Service from its earliest days. Instead of a poster stating that invalids need not apply, it is perhaps time to put out a call for only the best of the best. The resource deserves nothing but the best, after all.

While much remains to accomplish, in civil rights as well as in restoring the Forest Service image to that of a conservation leader, hundreds of unsung leaders within the agency carry on the work that continues to

Discussion of options for reducing mortality in whitebark pine, Bridger-Teton National Forest.

satisfy, in places that will never stop providing inspiration. The Forest Service has a foot in each of the two centuries of its existence; one is firm, bolstered by long experience, while the other is uncertain. Wilderness rangers clear trails with double-bits and crosscut saws, packing their gear for ten-day hitches into some of the most remote country remaining in the lower 48 states. This is the ongoing reality of work in the Yellowstone region, not part of a romanticized past. Many of the people doing this work are women. All of them are proud to know how to throw a box hitch and shoe a mule.

The future is less concrete, and increasingly worrisome, as the Forest Service attempts to respond to the many pressures facing it. But the magnificent country that impels young people to seek work for the agency endures. Wild country will endure as a treasure we hold in common, conserved and managed for the benefit of all, as long as the American people recognize its value.

Green River Lakes and Squaretop Mountain. Bridger Wilderness, Bridger-Teton National Forest.

21

A WORD FOR THE WILD, IN CLOSING. For much of the nineteenth century our government vigorously sponsored liquidation of the public domain, delivering vast acreages to the railroads and all but begging each prospective homesteader to claim his quarter-section. By the end of the 1800s a new idea had taken root, that of holding land in common for future generations. During Congressional debates over a park proposed for a district in the Rocky Mountains known as John Colter's Hell, naysayers predicted that it was so distant from civilization that no one would ever go there. As if to prove them wrong, Gilded Age ladies and gents of distinction sat behind smoke-belching steam engines for days, and wedged themselves into dusty mule-drawn stagecoaches, to enjoy an adventure in Yellowstone. Americans of their day had seen how quickly they could deplete the seemingly inexhaustible, from white pine forests in the upper Midwest to forty million bison on the Great Plains. By 1872, when Yellowstone became the world's first national park, the spark of stewardship in the collective psyche had grown into a small bright flame.

The region once called Colter's Hell is now known as the Greater Yellowstone Ecosystem and is listed as a UNESCO World Heritage Site. This matchless land of grizzly bears and geysers is held in high esteem by people around the world for reasons that would baffle the Forty-Second Congress of 1872.

Born of the same nascent conservation spirit that spawned the national park system, the Forest Service observed its centennial in 2005. The agency was under attack from the very branch of government that conceived it. Disguised with a bewildering array of euphemisms—downsizing, rightsizing, streamlining, out-sourcing—the fundamental agenda remained clear: to privatize the public land. This was no reprise of the homestead era with its opportunities for common folk to create a better life. An order

Old Faithful, Yellowstone National Park.

from the Agriculture Department in 2003 directed the Forest Service to find eighty million acres, along with some "unnecessary" historic ranger stations, to place on the auction block in order to boost federal revenue. Who besides well-funded land developers could afford to offer bids?

That effort was one of a series of attempts to divest citizens of their legacy by selling it or giving it away or turning its operation and management over to the private sector. These schemes have come and gone for decades, and each time, citizens rise up to vehemently resist the conversion of our national forests into Smokey Bear Golf and Tennis.

We do so to prevent the destruction of what is priceless: the wild earth that has been our home since the beginning of time. To prevent the ingrained American values of private rights and the profit motive from running roughshod over another set of values we hold dear: concern for the greater good, a sense of responsibility to the community for the benefit of all. And perhaps most importantly, to prevent another cycle of conversion of what can never be replaced by what is ordinary and uninspiring. The woodlots where we played as children are gone, traded for yet more housing developments, big-box shopping centers, and pavement. Where did the animals who lived there go? What became of our imaginations after the woodlots could no longer give us the raw materials for stories?

The chance to grow up playing in the woods without fear of human predators is unavailable to many of our children these days. But we have saved for them the national forests and other public places where they might taste the freedom of the kind of childhoods we enjoyed. In a land untrammeled by humans, a child may still feel the wonder of deep natural quiet or a star-filled night sky, believing he is the first person to stand on a wild, unnamed peak.

The wild helps keep alive our capacity for awe, humility, and empathy. Like the name of God to the ancient Hebrews, the essence of wilderness is something we cannot capture, describe, or fully understand. Yet, we know it when we experience it, and whether we bring back memories of sublime beauty or a narrow escape, these are the memories we keep for life.

One day in the Gros Ventre Wilderness many years ago, I startled a volunteer trail worker with my use of an uncommon word. In a soft southern accent, he tried to express the yen that had drawn him from Georgia to Wyoming to spend a summer repairing forest trails for sixteen dollars a

Pinedale District wilderness staff Cindy Stein, packing into the Bridger Wilderness, Bridger-Teton National Forest.

The author with Jackson Ranger District wilderness staff, Linda Merigliano.

day. Beyond the benefits of passing a season in wild country, he felt an urge toward service.

"Volunteering is something you just ought to do," he began. "It's a duty, I don't know, it's . . . "

"Citizenship," I offered.

He stopped. "I haven't heard that word since I was in the second grade."

I nodded. Until the word bubbled up into my conscious mind, I hadn't either, but it was the exact word that we had both been looking for. Citizenship was one of the points on which we second-graders were marked, and a category of achievement for which I once earned painted beads from the Campfire Girls. Back then it meant compliant behavior in the classroom or polishing one's saddle shoes before heading off to school. The volunteer trail worker and I understood it differently as we spent the day sawing deadfall and refreshing water-bars, sweating and laughing and pausing to admire the limestone cliffs towering above a field of wildflowers. How different that workday felt from the one before, when I'd banged for hours at a computer keyboard on yet another budget report. Compared to that cheerless exercise in bureaucratic busywork, this form of citizenship was play.

Americans are easily absorbed by the next new mobile device or recreational toy, but sometimes we must return to our source. That the forests will endure to offer their magnificence to coming generations is a cause worthy of vigilance and devotion. These United States are blessed by public land, where the beauty of nature and the chance to get outdoors is available to all citizens regardless of social station. In the Greater Yellowstone Ecosystem people can watch a grizzly bear glissading down a snow bank, or hear the distant howl of a wolf pack, or commune with a ground squirrel beside the boardwalk at Old Faithful. Here we experience the enduring wild, and where the wild endures we touch our deepest selves, and the deepest connections we have with our precious blue planet.

It has been fifty years since the passage of the Wilderness Act, and a couple of generations since the time when Americans were feeling generous enough to set aside land and resources for the future. It is hard to imagine such legislation passing these days, and hard to envision a public that would rise up to demand it. The history of the Wilderness Act, though the bulk of it took place when I was a child, lies fresh in my mind.

In 1964, the vocabulary of the Wilderness Act attempted to distill the essence of what was wild, with words like untrammeled, unconfined, and primitive. It spoke with eloquence for the value of the wild, while leaving to the future a quandary that had accompanied most of this nation's history in its relationship to our wild heritage: shall we appreciate wild nature as it is or conquer and subdue it, turning it to service toward our purposes? Can we do both?

In the seventeenth century, the vast wilderness of this continent frightened the British colonists, eager to transform their new surroundings into a facsimile of the gentle, long-subdued landscapes they left behind. But wilderness also helped form our national identity and transformed our ideas of scenic beauty, stewardship, and the place of humans in the grand scheme of creation. In the surviving journals of colonists, and of the first white families to travel west of the Mississippi in covered wagons, I have run across passages of awe and inspiration. I expected those pioneers to find the Great Plains boring and monotonous, and the arid lands farther to the west a vision of hell. Certainly many place names attest to such comparisons. Yet the diaries recorded joy over the unexpected beauty and abundance of the places those people encountered. Crossing the American wilderness, they had embarked upon the adventure of their lives.

Megan and Katie Harris sharing a sisterly moment in the wilderness after climbing the Sleeping Indian, Gros Ventre Wilderness, Wyoming.

Wilderness continues to challenge us with ideas that do not come naturally to a people who prize innovation and utility, private rights and profits. We are the children of pioneers and the boosters of Manifest Destiny, while the notion of wilderness preservation is all about restraint. The Wilderness Act says it this way: "In order to assure that an increasing population, accompanied by expanding settlement and growing mechanization, does not occupy and modify all areas within the United States and its possessions, leaving no lands designated for preservation and protection in their natural condition, it is hereby declared to be the policy of the Congress to secure for the American people of present and future generations the benefits of an enduring resource of wilderness."

Five decades after the Wilderness Act was passed, its architects have passed on. People have become increasingly estranged from this enduring resource. Our population is twice what it was in the 1960s and our means of occupying land and using it seem to know no bounds. Will Americans always believe in the need for self-restraint?

Before the ink from Lyndon Johnson's fountain pen had dried, we were violating the spirit of the Wilderness Act, if not by expanding settlement and growing mechanization (though those certainly played a part), by already having modified all areas within the United States, even the remote districts of Alaska. Airborne pollutants traveled the globe in a few hours, settling onto ground lichens that concentrated it. Noticeable climate change had commenced by the 1960s, and its effects were increasingly manifest in the Arctic. Pristine lakes had become acidified by industrial pollutants hundreds of miles upwind, while weeds replaced native plant species on which the wildlife depended.

Debates over wilderness stewardship have no definitive answers, for regardless of the science brought to bear, the decisions we make come down to a matter of human values. All I can do is hold each argument, however small and trivial the subject, up to the light of the Wilderness Act. Should rock climbers be allowed to leave bolts on rock faces? Should mountain bikes and other non-motorized wheeled vehicles be allowed? What about cell phones, GPS units, or whatever is next on the technological horizon? What will happen to the opportunity for challenge and personal adventure if gadgets make wilderness travel ever more safe and predictable? Does anyone care if the opportunity for adventure becomes more contrived than real?

As the National Wilderness Preservation System enters its second half-century, the ongoing assault on public wild lands continues. With gasoline

Celebration of the Wilderness Act's fortieth anniversary, at the Murie Center, Grand Teton National Park. Flo Shepard, center, is entertaining the crowd with a story.

prices ever in question, some people are convinced that we have a national imperative to drill for energy resources in places set aside for wilderness and wildlife. Western states and their attorneys continue to challenge the Roadless Area Conservation Rule in an effort to prevent further wilderness designation.

Wilderness is increasingly seen as nothing more than a scenic recreation area by people who expect it to be managed for their comfort and convenience. Visitors unprepared for the rigors of backcountry travel have learned to employ their mobile telephones and dispatch a helicopter to pluck them from whatever peril they have gotten into. What this trend might mean in terms of how we see ourselves and our relationship to the wild is suggested in a sample of comments made on trailhead registration sheets by backpackers returning from Wyoming's Bridger Wilderness.

"A small deer came into my camp and stole my bag of pickles. Is there a way I can get reimbursed? Please call."

"Trails need to be wider so people can walk while holding hands."

"All the mile markers are missing this year."

"Please avoid building trails that go uphill."

"Too many bugs and leeches and spiders and spider webs. Please spray the wilderness to rid the area of these pests."

"I was shocked at how steep the drop-offs are. Can't you put a safety net on the cliffs in case someone falls?"

"Chair lifts need to be in some places so that we can get to wonderful views without having to hike to them."

"The coyotes made too much noise last night and kept me awake. Please eradicate these annoying animals."

"Man always kills the things he loves," wrote Aldo Leopold in his classic *A Sand County Almanac*. "And so we the pioneers have killed our wilderness. Some say we had to. Be that as it may, I am glad I shall never be young without wild country to be young in. Of what avail are forty freedoms without a blank spot on the map?"

As a new generation of men and women take on the mantle of leadership within the Forest Service, it is my hope that there will always be a national forest system to serve people's spiritual needs: affordable campgrounds and roadside camps where they can camp on their own; well-maintained trails and places one can wander off alone and find respite from the noise and stress of the daily commute. With the Wilderness Act fifty years old

Inscription on the Roosevelt Arch, north entrance to Yellowstone National Park.

and the national forest system twice that, it is easy to take these gifts for granted. If future generations no longer value them, we can be sure of one thing: they will find their way to the auction block.

Share a special public place with a friend, listen with rapture to a child telling about an excursion into the forest, pick up a scrap of trash or plant a tree. There are as many ways to contribute to the greater good as there are people to do it, and by each following his inclinations we cover all the bases. This little strand of time we call a lifetime is a precious gift, ours to inhabit and to make our own. As we benefit from experiences, mentors, and places that have inspired us, there comes a time for each of us to fill the elder's chair, to consider our core principles and pass along our wisdom and our stories.

My story is nothing new, only my particular rendition of the oldest story of all—the quest for understanding, for consequence and meaning. With each act of service I peel another layer away, coming closer to the core, fueled by the hot fire in the heart that says *This Matters*. Each time I introduce another person to a favorite untrammeled place or a delicate wildflower, I shine a light on the satisfying depth of experience that accompanies reflective time outdoors. With hearts enflamed, we add our voices to a government of the people. People who speak for the freedom of the wild and the importance of the common, greater good, in the language of abundance and renewal.

Acknowledgments

Thanks to the dedicated employees of the USDA Forest Service who work tirelessly to provide service to citizens and stewardship for our precious national forests. Thanks to those who kept me sane and laughing during times of discouragement in the thirty-plus years I worked for the agency. Thanks especially to those mentioned in the book, for you are the ones who helped tell this story. Thanks to my husband, Don Plumley, who shared these experiences with me and listened to me griping about work for over thirty years.

The members of my longtime writing group read some of the essays that found their way into this book and gave me years of encouragement: Connie Wieneke, Tina Welling, Geenen Marie Haugen, sid woods, Susan Austin, and Kirsten Corbett. Special thanks to Tina, who read early drafts of this book and gave me valuable feedback.

The Jackson Hole Writers Conference, an annual event, was helpful for me. Its faculty and guests provided useful comments on various works of nonfiction, and the conference always challenges me to improve my craft.

Parts of this book appeared, in different form, in the following publications:

Chapter 5 includes excerpts from "Grizzly Bear," from the anthology *American Nature Writing*, Oregon State University Press, 2000.

Chapter 9 includes excerpts from "After the Mountain Men," from *Lifeboat: A Journal of Memoir*, Spring 2003.

Chapter 10 includes excerpts from "Into the Light," from the anthology *Women Runners*, Breakaway Books, 2001.

Chapter 14 includes excerpts from "Gathering Blackberries," from *Open Windows 2005*, Ghost Road Press, August 2005.

Chapter 15 includes excerpts from "Beyond Thunder Mountain," from the anthology *Ring of Fire: Writings from Yellowstone*, Rocky Mountain Press, 2000.

Chapter 16 includes excerpts from "A Simple Gift of Beauty," from *Wyoming* magazine, July 1997.

Chapter 17 includes excerpts from "Most of All, the Quiet," from *Camas*, Winter 2005.

Chapter 18 includes excerpts from "Re-Creation," from the anthology *The Leap Years*, Beacon Press, 1999.

NAME INDEX

Note: Photographs are indicated by italic page numbers

N

Y